MW01199746

Picket Line

Tom McCarty

Copyright © 2020 Tom McCarty

All rights reserved.

ISBN: 978167643348

DEDICATION

This book is dedicated to Betty and Sara.
Without their support this story would never have
been written.

CONTENTS

FOREWORD

On February 9, 2000 the Engineering and Technical workers represented by the Society of Professional Engineering Employees in Aerospace (SPEEA), IFPTE Local 2001, at the Boeing company went on strike.

Approximately 18,000 men and women refused to cross the picket line. The strike lasted forty days and forty nights.

This was reported by the *Los Angeles Times* as one of the largest white-collar strikes in U.S. history

This is a story worth telling. Many of the names have been changed to protect the innocent as well as the guilty. Like they say, this is my story and I'm sticking to it.

Tom McCarty

Seattle, WA

CHAPTER 1

DAY ONE

In about five minutes I'm going to find out if 20,000 people are willing to walk off the job. I know I'll be going out, but I never thought it would come to this. When I got offered a job at Boeing 27 years ago I accepted in a heartbeat. I'd be making more money, they had great benefits and they would pay to move me, Betty, our four kids and their Newfoundland dog "Fang" from New Jersey to Seattle. What's not to like?

My watch shows 9:00 a.m. and it looks like all the engineers on my floor are heading for the door. I wasn't sure how many would join the strike but this looks encouraging. Thankfully it's not raining, and by now the sun will be up and at 40 degrees it's almost balmy. Wednesday is not a bad day to start a strike and some people think if we stay out until Monday we'll be looking good. Well, February is a short month and we're already in the second week, so maybe it won't be too bad and we can last to the end of the month.

Winters in Seattle are grim, sometimes you don't see the sun for weeks. It's particularly bad for us who work in the huge windowless caverns at Boeing because the sun isn't up when you go through the gate and it's already down at the end of the shift. That's why I suggested we go out at nine o'clock so everybody would show up at their usual time and we would all go out together in the light of day. There was a risk that only a few of us would walk out, but that's not what happened.

As it turned out they were streaming out of buildings all over Puget Sound. The next day the *Seattle Times* reported: "By Boeing's estimate, as many as 16,000, or 75 percent, of its engineers and technicians in the Puget Sound area walked off the job yesterday. That exceeded SPEEA's area dues-paying members, who number about 13,000." Those numbers did not include those on strike in Oregon, Utah, California and Florida. This was a good start.

Well, the fat was in the fire at this point and we weren't entirely sure how it would play out, but one thing was for sure, everybody was pissed, determined and elated all at the same time. We had been planning for this day so we had rallies scheduled near the major Boeing locations. In the previous weeks, we met with the local labor councils and got a lot of help putting these together. We had thousands show up for speeches and demonstrations and while this was all going on the picket lines were forming and people were showing up.

It took time to get through the parking lot. People were collecting in small groups and speculating about what happens next. From the size of the crowd heading for their cars, it was obvious that most of the SPEEA-represented employees had walked out. Some headed home, others to their favorite tavern and more than a few thousand in Renton showed up at the high school football stadium. The union had booked the stadium for a rally and by the time I got there, it was packed. We heard speakers from other unions and local labor leaders. I got to speak and the crowd was pretty enthusiastic. Then it was time to head for the picket line. I decided to start my first picket line tour at my regular work location, the Boeing Space Center in Kent.

The picket lines had started forming right at nine o'clock that morning. In the previous weeks, picket assignment cards were sent to all union-represented employees whether they were union members or not. Since union membership was voluntary it wasn't clear how many would strike. Membership typically was only 40% of the eligible employees. The contentious negotiations had driven up those numbers and as it turned out many of the strikers were not union members. Since people didn't have any particular place to be, we had a big turn out on the picket lines. The lines were starting to get organized but they had the appearance of a block party at each picket site. This was somewhat of a departure from the traditional, more disciplined blue-collar strikes. As it turned out this was to become a new model for grassroots management of a crippling strike against a major industrial corporation.

Our picket sites needed burn barrels. These have been used at picket sites for as long as anyone can remember. They are usually made from 55 gallon steel drums with the top removed and vent holes cut in the sides. I had volunteered to pick some up at the salvage yard. I had a small shop out behind my house and could cut the required vent holes. After hanging out at the Kent picket line for a while, I headed home to get my truck and a load of burn barrels while it was still light.

We're the big story

Even though it was starting to get dark I wanted to check the local news on TV. There we were at the top of the 5 o'clock news, "Boeing Engineers on Strike" and some video of the picket lines and rallies.

I flipped through the channels and all the local stations had coverage and commentary. This strike was starting out quite a bit differently than the classic blue-collar strike where the workers file out of the factory and throw up a couple of picket lines at the gates and march back and forth. We had set up more than 50 picket sites at dozens of Boeing buildings in addition to the three airports where Boeing delivered and serviced planes: Paine Field in Everett, Renton Municipal Airport in Renton and Boeing Field in Seattle.

How we got to this point was rather convoluted. The Society of Professional Engineering Employees in Aerospace (SPEEA) until about three months prior was an independent, unaffiliated union that was considered rather meek and mild, nerds basically. This was reinforced by the universal media coverage and opinion that this strike may last a few days at most and we were expected to tuck our tails between our legs and return to work by Monday. As it turned out, some Boeing spokesperson was quoted saying that they expected most of the strikers would return by Monday morning and that just fanned the flames. One expert after another recounted that in SPEEA's history there had been only one other strike and that was for one day.

Well, this was only Wednesday night and the first day of the strike so I headed back to the picket lines at the Space Center and started putting in my time. I was able to load six barrels and some firewood in the truck and headed back to Kent. I stopped at the first gate and set up the barrel and started the fire and left a small pile of wood. There was always a lot of conversation at every stop but not much new yet. We haven't even gotten through the first day. Four barrels and four hours later, I took the last two barrels down to Auburn and dropped them off at the first two picket sites I came to. Since it was getting late, again after two more barrels and two more hours, I thought I'd head home. I wanted to stop at the Kent lines since they were on the way and see how it was going.

Everywhere I stopped at a picket site people wanted to talk. Many recognized me and if not, I introduced myself. There were five elected negotiation team members representing the engineers and five members representing the technicians. When the ballots were sent out on the first contract offer we had included a strike authorization vote. The negotiation teams were authorized to call for a strike by over 75% of the vote. That's a sobering thought. The ten of us had the power to call a strike and shut down the Boeing company, and although no one really believed that was possible, as it turned out that's exactly what happened.

I was out on the line when the 11 o'clock news came on and Betty told me when I got home that we were still the top local story. There were videos of some of the picket lines and interviews with some of the strikers. Video from the day showed huge crowds streaming out of the Renton and Everett plants and there were some night scenes at a few picket sites. The comments from the strikers had a common theme. They were determined to take a stand against what was seen as a total lack of regard for their contributions to the success of Boeing. People were starting to say "We're here for as long as it takes" and from day one the momentum was building.

It was harder to get out the door than it looked

Although the ten of us had been given the authority to call a strike it would have been nuts to think that thousands of employees would walk off the job just because we thought that was a good idea. SPEEA was definitely not an old school, top-down driven union where the rank and file followed orders. In fact, most people still didn't think SPEEA was a "real" union at all.

Much of the discussion that first night of the strike was about how we were treated during our negotiations as compared to the Machinists. Last summer, the Machinists union was at an impasse with Boeing over the terms for their new contract. They threatened a strike, and with their history, this was no idle threat. At the eleventh hour Phil Condit, Boeing's top executive, met with the Machinists and a greatly improved contract offer including a 10% bonus was approved by the members. That really rankled lots of SPEEA members.

We were supposed to start the strike the previous week. After the members turned down Boeing's second offer the negotiation team and key SPEEA staff had a long, contentious meeting to decide if we were ready to call the strike. The members certainly seemed ready based on face-to-face meetings and interactions with hundreds of members. But the extensive survey data we collected was less than convincing. The best reading of the data was that a slim majority was willing to go out for up to a week.

What the hell? It was hard to square the survey data with the visibly increasing calls for action in the workplace. The fact that the second offer was rejected did prove the members were not willing to settle and at every meeting and rally, we had rammed home the point that the only way to get a better offer was to reject the second offer and to go out on strike.

The members had rejected the second offer and now the SPEEA staff and the negotiation teams discussed for hours when and how to call for the strike. The SPEEA Director, Charlie, repeatedly argued for a one week strike and pointed out that this was supported by the survey data that the majority of members were willing to go out for up to a week. Most of us were not persuaded that this would have any meaningful effect on Boeing. If we announced we were going out for a week they could plan for it and nothing would change. The counter to that is to call for an unlimited strike which is more common for an industrial union.

After more arguing back and forth, I finally said: "If we are going to ask the members to go out on strike, then we have to give them a chance to win. If we tell them and Boeing we're only going out for a week there is no chance we can win this. We have to give the members a chance to win."

There was a pause while the team thought about it and then Stan, our engineering team chairman, said, "We need to go out for as long as it takes." When Stan said that, I knew we were going out for as long as it takes. Finally, Charlie asked when should we call the strike, and I responded, "Let's all walk out together Thursday morning at nine."

This strike may be shorter than you thought

Since we were tech-savvy there was a lot of information being exchanged by email and a few websites. Most of our members had computers and were very familiar with the internet. There was no problem getting the word out that the strike was on. But the downside to that was it was very easy to send a lot of bogus information to big mailing lists.

Things started happening fast once we called for the strike. We notified the media and it was all over the news that we are going on strike Thursday, February 3 at 9:00 a.m. The next morning an email was sent out from SPEEA to the members stating the strike would be called for only one week. Since I was on the negotiating team my Boeing email inbox shot up to over 1,500 emails in a matter of minutes. Other team members had the same experience. I immediately sent out a response to all stating the message was sent in error. Later that morning SPEEA sent a notice stating the previous message, calling for a one week strike, was sent in error. This only reinforced the perception we didn't know what we were doing. While all this was going on the International Federation of Professional and Technical Engineers (IFPTE), the AFL-CIO International we had affiliated with in October, was called and they contacted the AFL-CIO and intervention was arranged.

On Wednesday, we received a letter from Richard Trumka, Secretary-Treasurer of the AFL-CIO, asking us to delay the strike and meet with Richard Barnes who was the Director of the Federal Mediation and Conciliation Service (FMCS). This was the nation's top labor mediator. Barnes called us and requested that we delay the strike until he could fly from Washington D.C. to meet with us in Seattle on Monday and Tuesday next week. This was all over the morning news as I drove into work Thursday, February 3. Of course, we had agreed to delay the strike and meet with Barnes. What choice did we have? We were between a rock and a hard place.

When I got to work I expected the worst. It appeared to members, media and management that we did not (as expected) have the courage to back up our talk. We said we would call the strike if Boeing's offer was rejected a second time. In everybody's mind, a "real" union would have been out the door back in December when the offer was first turned down by the members.

Well, we called for the strike to start and then we announced that the start of the strike was on hold, it was that simple. Many members were outraged, others were not. One member stopped me in the hall and said since we were asked to delay the strike by the country's top mediator we should listen. The opinion shared by many that day was that we still had a chance to negotiate a better deal.

Why shouldn't I come up there and rip your head off?

The negotiation team went back to the SPEEA office that morning to plan our next steps. The workplace was in turmoil and we needed to get out in front of the members. The staff started setting up lunchtime meetings so we could meet the members and give them updates and explain what would be happening with the federal mediator and answer their questions. In the last few months, we had lots of these negotiation update meetings. Usually, three or four people were there to answer questions on the process and details about the negotiations as well as strike preparations. We had so many requests and only two workdays before we met with the mediator that we were out mostly by ourselves. I got an assignment to head over to the customer service location for a lunchtime meeting in the cafeteria.

When I got there the place was packed and I'm sure there were 200 people jammed in there. I was hoping I had at least one staff person there for support but no, I was all alone. I had a fair amount of experience giving presentations and public speaking but not so much in front of what could be considered a hostile crowd. This was a hostile crowd in general but they were engineers and willing to listen to reason. I wanted to make an appeal to reason and explain how we got where we are and this would dampen the raw emotions and anger that were evident. I think the gentlest comment I heard as I worked my way to the front was "So why did you bastards back down and call off the strike?"

When I got to the front I knew I was going to stay calm and cool and walk them through the events that led up to this morning. I went back to the last negotiations with Boeing and the final offer. I told them I absolutely thought that this was the best offer we could get without a strike. I was asked why the negotiating team recommended the approval of such a crappy offer. I said we recommended that the members vote to accept unless they were willing to go out for as long as it takes, and yes that's what the members decided.

I also said we spent hours yesterday debating and finally agreeing to the request of the top federal mediator to give him the opportunity to get some movement out of Boeing. I appealed to their sense of reasonableness by asking, "Wouldn't we want to make every effort to find a solution, if we could, before we commit to drastic action?" I pointed out once we're out it's not going to be a stroll down the garden path. I also pointed out that when we rejected the last offer Boeing withdrew that offer and there was now no contract to vote on. Unless the federal mediator convinces Boeing to make another offer we will have to strike to bring them back to the negotiating table.

I went into a lot of details about those final negotiation sessions and then asked the group if they had any questions. One big guy stepped forward and asked, "Tell me why I shouldn't come up there and rip your head off?"

This guy looked like an NFL defensive tackle, only bigger. You could hear a pin drop in that cafeteria. I paused for a few seconds and said, "I'm glad you asked me that question and the reason is that I'm on your side. In these negotiations, I'm working for you. I've been coming to work here for 27 years and I've taken just as much crap from Boeing as anybody in this building. I want to be treated with respect and that isn't happening at the negotiation table. The only way we're going to get a fair contract is by sticking together and not giving up. I'm not ready to give up, are you?"

That seemed to break the tension and the crowd was willing to listen and have an honest discussion. There were a lot more questions after that, and they were from people who were determined to do what it takes to get a fair contract. When I left I was hoarse from all the talking since I was on my feet and talking for two solid hours.

Day One wraps up

It was about 2 a.m. when I was finally heading home and I was hoarse again since at every picket site people wanted to talk about what happened and what to expect. Truthfully, I wasn't sure what to expect since we're breaking a new trail. Nobody had ever started a strike like this but we had prepared as best as we could and it was already showing.

The picket sites were well-staffed and people were in good spirits. Of course, it was only the first night. Everybody knew what they needed to do. We had picket captains assigned to four-hour shifts and they all had cell phones provided by SPEEA. We had our Seattle and Everett headquarters open and staffed 24 hours and they wouldn't close until the strike was over. We also started regular welfare checks about every four hours at each picket site and started hauling coffee, tea, hot chocolate and whatever snacks we could scrounge up. The next day we started handing out one-page strike news to keep people informed. The picket sites were easy to find since they all had a brightly lit burn barrel.

One last thing, since we had gone to all the local fire departments and police stations to inform them of the pending strike there were no problems on the line. In fact, the Kent police lieutenant I talked with suggested he would have a few extra patrols at night just to make sure everybody was safe. That's not surprising because back then every family had some relatives that worked at Boeing one time or another. It really was family.

CHAPTER 2

FAILED NEGOTIATIONS

Driving home from the line that first night gave me a chance to think about how this all played out. Some of us were new to this and the others had been through negotiations a few times before. The union side had been preparing for months. We had conducted several surveys to help us understand members' interests and priorities. We also brought in outside experts on benefits and medical plans to help us analyze Boeing's offer. The team also had attended a number of workshops taught by professionals in labor contract negotiations.

The negotiations were scheduled to take place over a three-week period at the Red Lion Hotel across from Sea-Tac Airport. The negotiation meetings were very formal, the company and union sat at a long conference table. There were about sixteen people on each side. The company sat on one side and we sat on the other, and yes we had assigned seats. Support people, both company and union sat along the walls on their own side. I sat at the end since I was the lowest ranking union guy which also meant I didn't get to say much. It was the same for the company. I sat across from the lowest ranking Boeing guy and he didn't get to say much either.

The negotiations kicked off with presentations by the company and union and then we went through the contract details section by section and line by line. When things got really technical, like the details of the medical plans, the main table meeting would adjourn and a smaller group would meet separately and if they agreed on proposed changes, that would be brought back to the main table. This was a slow deliberate process but progress was being made. We had been at this for over two weeks and we were expecting the company to present the contract offer. Once that was done it was expected they would hold back a few dollars, and we would wrangle out the last few dollars they were willing to give up. That was the typical outcome for Boeing and SPEEA negotiations. In contract negotiations, the company will typically offer a final bump up to the contract if the union team will recommend the offer to the members and give it the hard sell.

Can you say regressive bargaining?

Two days before we were scheduled to wrap up negotiations we were expecting the company to make a formal contract offer. We met after lunch at the main table and when the Boeing people filed in it was obvious that something had changed. I had gotten to know the lowest ranking Boeing guy who sat across from me over the last few weeks but when he sat down he avoided eye contact. The smiles and light-hearted bantering were also gone on the company side. The other telling sign was that they came into the conference room together in a single file and quietly sat down.

The Boeing spokesperson announced that the company was ready to present this contract offer and their lawyer handed it across the table to our lawyer. At the same time, one of the company staffers was giving each of us a copy of the thick document from a large cardboard box. We all started to scan the offer for the key features of money and benefits. It was immediately clear to all of us. This offer was completely different from what we had been working on for the last two and a half weeks.

We immediately adjourned for a caucus in our private suite. We divided up the offer into sections and gave each section to a small team for a painstaking review. What we're looking at rescinded all previous agreements and reduced salary pools, added insurance premiums and lowered pension benefits with a new pension plan. In collective bargaining language, this is called "regressive bargaining." One way to look at it is, the longer you bargain the worse the offer gets.

This was a total surprise to us and we probably should have seen it coming but we didn't. The Machinists had gotten what was considered a good contract the previous summer. The Machinists had a history of going out on strike if they couldn't get what they thought was fair. That threat certainly helped in getting an eleventh-hour settlement for them. With our history, that is no history of hardball labor negotiations, it looked like we were screwed.

Prior to the start of the formal contract negotiations, we had prepared a detailed line-by-line proposal for the new contract. Although realistically a company would never accept the initial union position, it does serve to state what labor's priorities are for the current negotiations. We prepared a detailed summary of our proposal and had presented it to our members and got a large turnout for a meeting in Seattle Center just before the start of negotiations.

The company's final offer, which we carefully reviewed, fell far short of any of our goals. It was an understatement to say we would have a big problem recommending this, much less showing it to the members. There was nothing left to do but to focus on the big issues and go back to the table and push back — hard.

When we returned to the big conference room once again, we sat in our assigned places and Charlie went down the short list of the unacceptable takeaways in the company proposal. The Boeing spokesman was the only one to respond and his answers were short and direct. The substance of the company position was that times were changing, market pressures demanded cost-sharing for employee benefits and the compensation package offered was competitive.

The afternoon session was becoming more unpleasant and tempers were growing short so we adjourned early and headed back to our suite. We were there until late at night going over our options and trying to develop a strategy to get some movement out of Boeing. We all went home to sleep on it and would reconvene early in the morning.

The next morning, as we reviewed the options, was the first time I heard the strike option discussed but we decided to hold that back since we really didn't have much credibility in that arena.

When we met with the company there was no meaningful movement. The company eventually proposed a few small improvements if the negotiation team would accept the offer and recommend approval to the members. This was a typical way for management to wrap up negotiations. That's when it all fell apart and got ugly. It quickly degenerated into a shouting match. We proceeded to express our outrage and colorful opinions but I will admit almost everyone on the management side kept quiet and stared straight ahead.

Nothing productive happened that last day, it was very clear to us that the company felt they could force us to accept this contract. They were in the position of power and were convinced that we did not have a militant membership willing to walk the line to force the company to provide a better offer. As we left the conference room one of the engineering managers that I had known said to me, "Tom, you're not representing the members' interests. This is a good offer and it will be approved by the vast majority of the members."

The following day at union headquarters we had to get the offer out to the membership. The negotiation team and staff put together a summary of the offer and prepared for the afternoon Council meeting. The news of the bad offer had already circulated, and the meeting room was electric with the tension. We presented the offer, handed out summaries and answered questions. The council formally rejected the offer and called for a strike vote.

The next morning we prepared the ballot package. The ballot package included our recommendation for rejection and also asked for strike authorization. The ballots were sent to every member, and they had two weeks to cast their votes. During those two weeks, we had many meetings, and the anger over what was perceived as an insulting offer started to build. The fact that it was generally seen that the Machinists had gotten a good contract only fueled the fire.

The ballots came in quickly and piled up at our post office box. When it finally came time to count them there were thousands and thousands. The results surprised everyone. The Boeing contract offer was rejected by over 98% of the members and the strike authorization vote passed by over 85%.

This was big news in the local press and every TV station carried it on the 11 o'clock news that night. Now that we absolutely knew how the members felt, the challenge was to figure out a way to do something about it.

Will we strike or not?

Although there was an outcry from some members to call a strike, realistically that wasn't going to happen — yet. The team and staff had long meetings trying to find a path forward. It was December 3, and Boeing has a paid week shutdown between

Christmas and New Year's Day. It wouldn't make any sense at all to be on strike during paid holidays. The other big factor was, of course, we had no planning in place or experience to conduct a strike on this scale.

We decided to move forward the way engineers think, let's keep all the options open. The desired outcome was to get Boeing back to the table and get a better offer but their initial position was, "You got our offer, take it or leave it." So we reached out to the IFPTE and the local labor councils to ask for help in planning a strike. We started holding lunchtime meetings in the workplace and talking to the press at every opportunity. The goal was to ratchet up the pressure on Boeing. We started to get some traction and were contacted by the local office of the Federal Mediation and Conciliatory Service (FMCS) since it was their charter to mediate labor disputes. Our job was to elevate this dispute. Their job was to make it go away.

After a few weeks, it started working, and the FMCS got Boeing to agree to reopen negotiations. The first meeting was scheduled for early January after the holiday break. The strike preparations were now a full-time job for a few union committees and staff, and we were getting a lot of help from our labor contacts. The tone in the workplace was becoming more militant. But it should be clear that there still was a lot of skepticism from members, management and the press as to the ability of our mild-mannered union to actually go out and stay out on a serious strike.

We met with the local federal mediators in the second week of January 2000 before meeting with Boeing. In fact, they met separately with us and the company prior to meeting face-to-face. The atmosphere was formal but tense. Boeing had a new offer and introduced it with the remarks that since SPEEA had been complaining that the Machinists' offer was better than the SPEEA offer they had tailored the new offer to align with the contract the Machinists had accepted.

They then proceeded to walk through the proposal section by section. It did appear that there were some modest improvements but there also were some additional reductions in benefits. We were provided copies of the new proposal and we adjourned to our meeting room to review the details. One thing that immediately stuck out was that the company for many years had provided life insurance for all the salaried employees which had always provided 2.25 times the employee's annual salary. In the new proposal, this was reduced to a flat $32,000. We thought this was a cheap shot. The cost savings to the company were lost in the noise. The optics of it was clear to us — another stick in the eye to demonstrate their power in these negotiations. After hours of review and analysis, we called it a night.

When we think about the whole offer, it's hard not to personalize it. A sense of mean-spiritedness was just beneath the surface. A good example of that was the removal of the Long Term Disability Plan. This plan was an optional group insurance plan paid for by the employees. This plan would pay employees 80% of their salary for up to two years if they became injured or disabled and were unable to work. It cost the employee about $30 a month. Since Boeing sponsored this as a group plan it was very affordable and cost them almost nothing. (The *Seattle Times* pointed that out in a Boeing/SPEEA Negotiations update on February 8, 2000.)

The next day we're back in our meeting room early and decide to press even harder for the best offer we can get. The mediator met with us again before sitting down with the company and gives us the story that Boeing has put every dollar they can into the offer. He goes on to remind us that any strike could be long and he didn't see any history of that militancy with SPEEA. This is the message in one form or other that shows up everywhere, even in our own ranks. The mediator and many others want us to accept the offer and move on. More and more other members are deciding they're not going to accept any sucky Boeing offer.

Well, it's back to the table and once again the company files in and takes their seats. There is very little eye contact and Boeing's chief negotiator goes through a summary of the new offer. There are some possible improvements but with all the new language it's hard to tell how much money has been added. It is clear that this is still a loss compared to the last contract. We again hear how we are being unrealistic, the current market forces require a lean approach and finally, this is a competitive offer and the company has thoughtfully considered our needs. We are not impressed and take our copies back to our meeting room to do a detailed analysis.

When we return we begin to bore down on the many remaining issues but the company is getting impatient with the debate. Their response is they have put additional money into the offer. We counter that although our analysis shows very little has been added our major concerns are not addressed. After some unproductive back and forth the mediator calls for a recess. During the recess, the mediator met separately with the company and then comes back and meets with us. The mediator wants us to realize that the company feels it has gone far beyond its original position and has made considerable concessions in the current offer. He wants us to give this careful thought in our deliberations. He also suggests that if we do not agree to take this offer out to the members with our recommendation to accept the company may withdraw the offer.

The final session with Boeing went exactly like the mediator hinted at. The company was done with us, that was clear. I definitely got the impression that at that point we could take the offer or not because they had their own plans. They made it simple for us, we were told that they put in everything possible and this offer was made contingent on our recommendation to the members. If we were not able to do that, the offer was withdrawn and we had until close of business today to decide.

That put us in a tough spot because if we walked out without the offer for the members to vote on that means we had no labor contract since our current contract had only been extended for the duration of the extended negotiations and ratification vote. What that means is if there are no contract protections then ultimately — no union. This was hardball and we didn't have much choice. We took out the contract under those terms and the vote was next.

The second vote

We came out of the meeting and brought the offer to the union council and laid it all out for them and they agreed with us. The offer was going out for a mail vote and we would have the results in about two weeks. We immediately prepared a summary and talking points and got ready to take this show on the road to the members.

Thanks to the internet we were able to get the information out to members pretty quickly. The next day we started lunchtime meetings and they were packed.

The members who came to the meetings were not happy and the dissatisfaction with the second offer seemed to grow exponentially with each meeting. Outside these meetings, things were generally quiet. But inside the union hall, things were busy, we quickly spread the word that if this offer was rejected we would call the strike. In the meetings I spoke at, I got a lot of push back on our accepting a crappy offer. I didn't want to be on the defensive, but it's true that I signed the letter sent to every engineer stating I recommended the offer. I told the members at every meeting, "I recommend you accept this offer unless you are willing to go out on strike for as long as it takes because that is the only way you'll get a better offer." As it turned out my qualified recommendation was not acceptable to Boeing, but what the hell that's the way it was.

The two weeks gave us, the union staff, union officers and volunteers time to organize the strike preparations and work out the details. It was coming together and we thought we would be ready if the contract was rejected. The awareness of the contract vote built up to a fever pitch in the workplace. Hand-drawn signs and placards started showing up on the braver members' desks and cubicle walls. The message was pro-union and pro-strike but nothing official from the union other than the "We need a fair contract now" buttons and stickers printed by the union when negotiations kicked off. Most managers turned a blind eye to this lobbying, some were sympathetic since if we could push back on health care premiums and get bigger salary pools they would benefit as well based on past company practice.

Finally, it was time to count the second vote. The union hall is packed and the Tellers are counting the ballots. They are in a separate area roped off in the big meeting room. We can see by how they are stacking the counted ballots that this is going to be close. The press is there and the tellers are very meticulous with the ballots. There is no rush and the count is proceeding very orderly. Technical people like to be precise and we want confidence in the outcome whatever that may be. The ballots are all accounted for and the totals are carefully cross-checked. The head teller heads up to the podium to announce the results.

The contract is rejected by both the Engineers and the Technicians for a second time. We are going out on strike. we send out the message to all the members that the strike would start at 9:00 a.m. Thursday, February 3, 2000.

We get a call from the Feds — Wait hold off!

As soon as we announce the strike is on we get a faxed letter from the AFL-CIO that the top federal mediator is asking us to delay the walkout. This was also passed on to the press and local media. All the local TV stations announced that the White House was intervening to avert a strike. It was apparent that this was orchestrated by some of the union leadership here and in Washington D.C. The pressure was enormous and we really didn't have much choice. We agreed to hold off the strike and meet with the federal mediator and Boeing on Monday and Tuesday next week.

It was pure chaos in the workplace Thursday and Friday. Once again the image of SPEEA as a weak and ineffective union was reinforced. There were spontaneous rallies and demonstrations although most members thought it was reasonable to meet with Boeing in mediated talks. There was at least one altercation by outraged members at the union halls that almost erupted in violence.

During this time the negotiation team and key staff

had a conference call with our international president and Richard Trumka, then Secretary-Treasurer of the AFL-CIO. The leadership in Washington D.C. was still skeptical of our ability to successfully conduct the strike. The fact was our own polls showed barely half the members were willing to stay out for a week. I had argued that despite this, based on my 27 years of experience working with these members they would do whatever it takes to win this strike. In the end, Trumka said if we went out the AFL-CIO would support us. That meant all organized labor would support us and that was important.

On Monday morning February 7, we met with Richard Barnes the top federal mediator. He was appointed by President Clinton and confirmed by the U. S. Senate and he had flown out from Washington D.C. to Seattle to mediate this labor dispute. We were definitely in the big league now.

He met with us for several hours and listened to our grievances then after lunch he met with Boeing. When he came back to our meeting room he carefully explained how this process works. He is looking for some movement on each side and trying to find some common ground. He told us his job is to prevent strikes and if one side or the other gets the short end of the stick it really doesn't matter to him. He advised us to think about it long and hard that night and consider the harm that could result to our members if we proceeded with the strike.

First thing Tuesday morning he met with us and advised us he didn't think the company was going to budge one inch. He said he'll give it one more try with Boeing and gave us each a small sticky note and told us to write our "must-have" demands on the note and to write large since his eyesight wasn't that good. He headed over to the company's meeting room with the sticky notes in his hand. He returned in about an hour and said he would like us all at the table again and see if we could work something out.

We all filed into the big meeting room and the union and company sat once again in our assigned places with Barnes at the head of the table. It was his meeting. He asked each side in turn what it would take to settle the dispute. It didn't go well and we were all done in a few minutes, voices were loud and tempers were short. The last thing I heard was "We're outta here" followed by "Don't let the door hit you in the ass."

Back in our room Barnes looked resigned and told us sometimes a strike just can't be avoided. He also told us that as engineers we're used to analysis and logical decisions based on facts and numbers. That time has passed and now it's become an emotional issue for both sides. He finally said all strikes have to end and when we're ready he will help us do that.

The past few days weren't wasted, the strike preparations and the members' resolve had reached a fever pitch. We're hitting the bricks at 9:00 a.m. tomorrow for as long as it takes.

CHAPTER 3

FIRST WEEK

On the second day of the strike, there is still some uncertainty as to how we will proceed. There is also a lot of enthusiasm and the picket lines are well-staffed. I loaded up some more 55 gallon drums and firewood in my truck and drove over to union headquarters. That became my usual routine. First thing in the morning I would check-in and find out what needed to be done that day. We were still setting up picket sites as Boeing opened new gates to avoid the picketers. We were already covering over 50 sites. I got a list of sites that didn't have burn barrels in the south end. Up north in Everett, there were other members doing the same thing.

I headed out to deliver the modified 55 gallon drums that were universally used at picket sites to the few new sites that still needed them. But inevitably I would pass a picket site that was up and running so I would have to stop and see how they were doing. I would pass along what I knew and get the latest news at that site. Although this slowed me down, it became normal for strikers to just stop by and spend some time at the picket sites whether it was their picket shift or not.

Since we were part of the AFL-CIO we had the full support of the labor community and it was beginning to show. One thing we found out was that Teamster drivers wouldn't cross our picket lines, so no deliveries to the Boeing plants. This was having an immediate big impact on Boeing. Everything from office supplies to parts needed to build airplanes was sitting in trucks and not being unloaded in the Boeing warehouses. It gets worse. Whole 737 airplane fuselages are shipped by rail from Wichita, Kansas to the Renton plant for final assembly. The Brotherhood of Locomotive Engineers and Trainmen won't cross our picket lines either. A few of our members were quick enough to recognize this and set up a picket line across the tracks. From then on we did this everywhere freight came in by rail to Boeing plants.

Boeing quickly responded to the truck freight holdups by setting up temporary drop-offs at isolated commercial warehouses. Thanks to the solidarity of our Teamster brothers and sisters as soon as they learned they were hauling freight for Boeing they'd give us a call so we could have our flying squad arrive in time to set up a picket line. I was on a few of those and it worked very well. We'd get a wave and a smile and the Boeing freight would stay on the truck and head down the road.

As I drove around the picket sites I was impressed by the positive attitude of the strikers. I'll call them all strikers from now on because I can't tell the union members from the non-members. When I left headquarters that morning I saw a few people signing up and paying their union dues, amazing, we're on strike and people are joining the union.

Settling in for the strike

All the sites were well-attended and mostly everyone was relaxed. I stopped at every site I passed and had a lot of good conversations and made new friends. Two days of the strike weren't enough time to prove we were going to "stay out as long as it takes." By the third day, the tone of the media was changing a little, although there was considerable doubt that we will last still evident in their coverage. There was a report that circulated that Boeing management expected a large number of the strikers would be back at work Monday morning.

The picketers were fewer at night and of course no kids and strollers like I would regularly see during the day. The weather the first two days was mild and no rain which helped with the initial turnout. As

I drove around to the sites at night the orange flicker of flames from the burn barrels provided a cheery atmosphere, it was getting colder at night, so people naturally congregated around the source of heat and light and passed the quiet hours in conversation.

I blame myself for the next development because I did place a burn barrel in front of Boeing Corporate Headquarters right in front of Boeing President Harry Stonecipher's second floor office window. When I was there that day I noticed a pickup truck with SPEEA strike placards taped to the doors and tailgate. I noticed this because it was impossible not to. This striker had mounted a large air horn on the ladder rack on the truck bed. This horn was almost as long as the ladder rack and he had jury-rigged it to run off a couple of scuba tanks. The striker would spend hours driving back and forth sounding that horn in front of Harry's office. Yes, it was loud and sounded like a diesel locomotive parked next to your house. Since it got dark by 4:30 p.m. the burn barrel was clearly visible when Harry looked out his window. I learned many years later from someone on the executive row at the time that Harry was in his conference room at a late meeting and pointed out the window at the glowing barrel surrounded by picketers and remarked, "Aren't those fires illegal?" I know somebody gave the EPA a call.

Ban the burn barrels

The next morning when I stopped by headquarters, Maria from the staff grabbed me and said we got a big problem. She handed me a letter from the Puget Sound Air Pollution Control Agency (EPA) advising SPEEA that the burn barrels were in violation of air pollution regulations and we would be subject to fines each day for every barrel with a fire. This was going to be very hard on the picketers when during the day it was rainy and cold and a hell of a lot worse at night.

The envelope from the EPA contained some literature and there was information on what type of fires were allowed. It turns out that open cooking fires are allowed and I suggested to Maria maybe we just need a bunch of sticks and lots of hotdogs. Well, after the eye-rolling from Maria, I re-read the information and found a possible solution.

The item that struck me was that all fires are allowed if they are in an enclosed stove with a chimney that exits the smoke 6 feet above the ground. It went on further to state these stoves can be home built. The staff was getting the word out to all the sites to quit burning in the barrels and started buying propane heaters to send out to the picket sites. I thought about it and told Maria I think I can come up with something.

Since I had nothing to work with left at home, I

headed down to the Kent salvage yard where I had previously picked up a dozen or so of the regular 55 gallon steel drums for the picket sites. Of course, I stopped by the main picket site in front of the Space Center in Kent. There was no fire in the burn barrel but since it was a mild day it didn't bother people much. It turned out that would change once it got dark.

When I got to the salvage yard the owner recognized me since I had made several previous trips. He actually said, "What's up Tom, you need more barrels for the strike?" That did catch me by surprise. We were only 3 days in so far but it seemed everybody was following the strike. Anyway, I told Dave the EPA had shut us down and I needed to figure out something that was totally enclosed. Dave responded, "Good luck with that and let me know if you need help."

As I looked around the yard I saw a large collection of clean 55 gallon drums and one caught my eye. It had a lid resting on top but not fully covering the opening. After studying it for a few minutes I thought this is enclosed, all I need is a way to open it to add wood and have a chimney for the smoke. I rolled 4 barrels and lids out to the front. Dave wished me well saying, "It looks like you found something and since you're a regular customer now, how does 5 bucks each sound? I'll give you the striker discount."

I loaded the barrels and lids in the truck and headed for Home Depot. There I picked up a pair of strap hinges. a gate latch, a 2 foot piece of 6 inch stove pipe and a box of #6 hex head sheet metal screws. When I got home I was ready to put together a home built enclosed wood stove with a chimney 6 feet above the ground. Luckily out in my shop, I had everything else I needed. My first attempt was sort of okay. I built a fire in it and it worked pretty well but it was kind of big. I had welded one barrel on top of the other, and added a feed door like a giant pot-bellied stove. It was dark by then so I closed the shop and headed back to the picket lines.

I went out to a few sites that night and saw the propane heaters in use. Not much light and less heat if two people were standing in front. It had started to rain lightly, typical Seattle drizzle, and it was pretty miserable for the picketers on duty that night. This was noticeably different from the previous night. People were scattered around, some had flashlights but the overall effect was dark and gloomy. This was reflected in the somber attitude of the strikers.

I got up early the next morning and loaded my first attempt at an enclosed stove and some firewood in the truck and headed for Kent. I went to the main gate site and unloaded the stove in a good spot. The picket captain came over and immediately knew what was going on. We got it set up on the sidewalk and I had remembered to bring a few bricks to set it on. We opened the door and with some newspaper and kindling got the fire going. A few strikers gathered around and some of them were stragglers from earlier when it was still dark. The verdict was immediate, we were back in business.

While I was hanging around with the picketers it dawned on me how to make this simpler. I needed to make these as fast as possible and the one I was looking at took too much screwing around and it was a pain in the ass to transport. Then in a flash of inspiration, I knew just how to do it. I left the strikers and said I'll be back when I have more of these. I went back to Home Depot and bought 4 pairs of strap hinges, and 8 pieces of 6 inch stove pipe. Then I went home to build four SPEEA stoves.

It turned out to be simple and quick. I cut the lids in half and screwed that to the top of the drum. Then I cut a 6 inch hole for the stovepipe in the top half of the drum and attached 2 sections of stove pipe using a simple flange joint. I attached the free half of the lid to the drum top with the strap hinges. Finally, I cut three 2 inch holes on the sides near the bottom then I screwed a rafter tie to the hinged lid for a handle and it was done.

I started a fire to test it out and it worked great. I gave Maria a call at the SPEEA office and told her I thought I had a solution and described it to her. She said she would like to call the EPA guy and see if we could get him to agree my stove meets all the requirements. While I was building the next three I got a call from Maria telling me the inspector would like to see what we got and he would be able to swing by the SPEEA office tomorrow morning about nine o'clock. I told Maria I'd be ready and would see her in the morning.

The SPEEA stove — Just in time

I got to work and finished the three stoves by later that night and started a fire in each so they wouldn't smell on the line like new steel always does when it's heated. That morning I loaded the truck with four finished stoves and some firewood and headed for the SPEEA office. I got there a little early and went in and found Maria and told her I was ready and four stoves were in the parking lot. She came out and said they looked like they met all the requirements on the EPA checklist. She was pleased I could come up with something so quickly, but I told her, "No problem, I'm doing this full time."

We were in the parking lot when the inspector showed up. We made our introductions and I took one of the stoves off the truck. He checked the stove carefully and remarked the design was very clever and the workmanship was good. I realized he was actually on our side when he looked at each of us right in the eye and said you won't have a problem with the Puget Sound Air Pollution Control Agency. He then offered his hand and smiled so we all shook hands. He said he would close the complaint when he got back to the office and drove off. We never did see or hear from him again. I had the distinct feeling he had a kid on the line in Renton or maybe Everett.

I took the four stoves to the Kent picket site to start exchanging them for the outlawed open barrels. While I was setting up the new stoves I would get help from the picketers. The word had already started spreading that new stoves were coming back. People were enthusiastic when I got the stove going. One immediate benefit was no matter which way the wind was blowing, the smoke never blew in your eyes. It was around lunchtime by then and one striker said, "Hey, I should have brought a pot of chili to set on there." I looked at him and then the hot flat top of the stove and said, "Of course, that's what it was designed for." Well, that's exactly what happened, people started showing up with pots and frying pans morning, noon and night. This was the stuff of legend. It seemed no strike had done this before but it became commonplace to see a coffee pot or scrambled eggs on the SPEEA stove at a picket site in the morning. I saw hotdogs boiling in a pot at lunch and stew in the evening.

I was setting up the next stove and I saw one of the guys I worked with come over to check out the stove. Morris had been on a late shift at the site and knew the value of the fires. He asked me if I built these and I said yes I just started yesterday and I've got a bunch more to make. Morris asked me if I could use some help as he's not very busy right now since he's not going to work. I knew Morris very well since we had been working together on the same project for a year. I immediately told Morris I would welcome his help and he got in the truck and we set up the last two stoves.

When we were done setting up the stoves we agreed to meet in the morning and get supplies to build six more SPEEA stoves. For the next week or so that was our routine. Some picketers came down from Everett to see what we were building and went back north to build some more. A few others built some and soon all the picket sites had environmentally friendly new SPEEA stoves.

One final note on the burn barrels. One of the open barrels we replaced early was the one in front of Harry's office at Boeing headquarters. The open barrels at some picket sites were still being used but we never heard squat from the Puget Sound Air Pollution Agency, it was a dead issue

By Sunday that first week, some amount of normal routine is settling in. Even though it was a short week we are starting to get a lot of food donations at the picket sites. People in cars and trucks pull over to the curb and roll down a window or open a door and hand over a dozen donuts (sometimes 2 dozen), a pizza or a bag of burgers. Sometimes they give us cash donations. People are doing the same thing at our Seattle and Everett union halls and more food is showing up in food bank quantities of non-perishables.

Harry was quoted by the press as saying that engineers should get over it, "Engineers are not the center of the universe." It turned out as far as Boeing was concerned, we pretty much were. We knew the kind of impact we were having because of all the connections we had inside the Boeing plants. We knew things were quickly grinding to a halt and Boeing management was also aware of how things were slowing down. A local news report quoted some Boeing executive saying they expected a lot of strikers to cross the line on Monday which happened to be February 14. Over the weekend it was mild and there were lots of families and parents pushing strollers. Most of the sites had a "Block Party" aspect to them. By the time we got to the first weekend things were sorted out and the picket lines were well-organized. Every major site had a burn barrel or SPEEA stove, a porta-potty, and a small picket captain shack to store supplies.

We got through the first week and the media picked up on it and we finally got some grudging respect. There were a few small crises but we worked through them. Most individuals were doing okay since nobody missed a paycheck yet. The advantage we have over the company is our agility and the fact we don't actually have a rigid chain of command. There are a lot of self-motivated activists out on the line and when they see something that needs attention they usually jump right in. Good ideas are recognized and spread by word of mouth.

CHAPTER 4

SECOND WEEK

Well, the word traveled through the lines over the weekend that the company expected large numbers of strikers to cross the line and return to work. Bright and early Monday morning there was a huge turnout at the picket sites. Since it was Valentine's Day the theme was "Bring your Sweetie to the picket line today!" People hung around until the late morning and the atmosphere was upbeat. There were not a lot of kids on Monday morning because it was a school day and it was kind of cold and raw for the younger ones. The media picked up on this and our credibility was growing.

I met up with Morris on the line and I had some stoves in the truck for us the deliver to the Auburn plant sites. We both wanted to check on how things looked there. The main gate in Auburn was located in a busy area with lots of traffic day and night. This was another great picket site for access and public exposure. We wanted that visibility because we realized just how important it was to connect to every other person who goes to work every day to make a living. When we got there we were recognized immediately, probably the SPEEA stoves in the back of the truck were a tip-off.

The old open barrels were still in use but we had a quick fix for that. Some of the picketers jumped up in the truck and unloaded two stoves. There was a big paved walkway, much bigger than a sidewalk. On each side of the Boeing entrance, the Auburn guys had set up a barrel and they were almost half a block apart. I had a shovel with me and had done this before. I just opened the stove lid and with the shovel gently tipped over the burning barrel and shoveled the burning wood into the stove. Closed the stove lid and it was done and took less than 2 minutes. I left the old barrel there and when it cooled down it became the picket site trash can. I got my broom and swept up the area and dumped the sweepings in the trash can. All the sites were kept clean and orderly, the picketers definitely took pride and ownership in the sites.

Keep the fires going

I was talking to a few of the picketers and I noticed a forklift zipping towards the gate from inside the property. The forklift had a skid tub of broken pallet wood. If you're not familiar with an industrial skid tub all I can tell you is they are big and will hold almost as much as a mini pickup truck. The driver waved at us and scooted right over to the stove, lowered the tub, backed the forks out, spun around and headed back through the gate — all in one continuous fluid motion like a ballet dancer. I have always had the greatest respect for the Machinists at Boeing. They are militant, they are strong and they are on our side.

Well, needless to say the free wood deliveries wouldn't last long but I did notice from time to time a few piles of broken pallets would appear outside the Auburn gates, especially during the third shift. The public support we got at the picket sites was amazing. People would regularly leave firewood and food for the strikers. More than once a guy would show up with a full truckload of dry split firewood. The next morning I was on the Kent site and I walked over a block to the gas station to get a cup of coffee. It was about 8 a.m. and the place was busy. I had my coffee in one hand and my picket sign in the other. When it was my turn at the counter as I was reaching for my wallet, I heard a loud voice behind me. I turned around and the third guy in line was a UPS driver. He called out, "Hey Buddy, I want to buy that coffee for you. If you guys let Boeing cut your health benefits, mine will be next."

There were actually some loud vocal approvals in that crowd of strangers. I loudly thanked him and he responded, "We're in the same fight!"

The picket sites were running more or less very smoothly. Morris and I kept busy all that week getting the new stoves out to all the sites in the south end. I'd check in each day at headquarters and get a list of sites that still needed the new stove. We got the main gates at all the Boeing sites taken care of pretty quickly. There were smaller sites at some isolated locations and seldom-used back gates on side streets that took a while to get to. These sites didn't have the big turnouts that the big sites had. I did feel a little sorry for those picketers but I admired their resolve, they were committed to picket every open gate where there was access to a Boeing plant.

I got a message that afternoon to deliver a stove to a new site. It was already dark when I got to the isolated site at a parts warehouse. There was very little going on after dark in this area, just rows of empty buildings. I saw a small group of picketers and they were carrying their signs and had flashlights and camp lanterns and that was it. As I pulled over I noticed a few kids which wasn't unusual since it was only around six o'clock. A few people came over to the truck and a boy about eight years old asked me if the stove in the back of the truck was for them. I said yes that's why I'm here and we unloaded it and found a spot to set it up.

When we got the fire going and were standing around the stove, I saw that it made a big difference. With all the issues that brought on this strike it would seem that having a fire at night would not be that important, but yet it was. The affinity we have for a glowing fire at night must be locked deep down in our DNA. Besides keeping wild animals at bay it does serve as a place to gather around and warm up. People had a lot of good conversations about the strike and what their expectations were. That shared experience is what developed into the solidarity that was going to keep this strike going. When I finally left after spending some time at this isolated site I noticed the young boy and a friend were standing next to the stove engaged in conversation and smiling.

I had a chance to run up to Everett this week and they have the most elaborate picket site I have seen yet. They have set up a big army tent with carpeting and couches on a large grassy strip across from the Everett main gate. At night they run their generator, power up the strings of lights and play rock music. They also usually have a couple of Weber grills going.

On the way to Everett, I stopped to check up on my college pal Doug who was now an engineer at Boeing in flight controls. He was on strike even though he wasn't a union member. I had called to let him know I was coming, so when I knocked on the door he opened it and handed me a SPEEA membership application and a check for his dues. The fact that he wasn't a member up to then wasn't an issue because I respected his choice. When he handed me the check he said, "I support what you guys are doing and it's time for me to join the union." He remained a member until the day he retired.

I asked him if he would like to go over the main Everett picket site with me. I planned to give the picketers an update from the south end. I suggested he could give them some information on the impact the DERs (Designated Engineering Representative) on strike were having on plane deliveries. He agreed, and when we got to the Everett site I found the picket captain and told him who I was and I also told him that Doug was a DER and we could give people an update and take questions if they would like. He jumped on that and we quickly assembled a crowd in front of their big tent. These guys have a PA system set up to play music but they also have a microphone on a stand ready for use. Most of the strikers knew what a DER was. They are engineers that are designated by the Federal Aviation Administration (FAA) to review flight worthiness documents and authorize the release of new airplanes.

Since almost every DER was on strike Boeing deliveries to their customers had slowed to a crawl and soon they would be halted completely.

Keeping it together — How do you organize 18,000 strikers?

We were coming up on our first full week (7 days) of the strike although the media universally called this the second week of the strike. The strike was developing a culture of its own. Many of us worked full time on keeping people informed and fixing problems. This was how we started the food banks. After a few days, we had started to accumulate a lot of non-perishable food donations. Since we had a regular service van visiting all the sites we just started sending the food donations back to headquarters in Tukwila and Everett. That quickly became a big pile of stuff all mixed together. Some of the staff and volunteers decided to get to work and create a functioning food bank. Once the food bank was organized and grocery bags were purchased we could start filling the bags with a reasonable selection of food items. The next problem was to connect the groceries with the strikers that could use them.

Our union had its own print shop which was a longstanding tradition in the labor movement but somewhat old fashioned lately. Robbi was the staff editor of our newsletter and the monthly magazine. She was also the office manager and the behind-the-scene jack of all trades. There's no doubt that Robbi made sure things that needed to get done, got done. Robbi created a daily one-sheet newsletter that was printed each day and stacks were placed in the service vans. This newsletter was called "Line on the Line" and a stack of them were at every picket site every day. This was one of the ways we were able to keep everybody informed about what was happing.

That second week we were not yet feeling the loss of our paychecks. Thursday that week was a payday and everybody on strike lost 2 days in the pay period, so we all got 64 hours of pay instead of 80 hours not counting any overtime. In two weeks it will be grim because that will be a zip paycheck for everyone. The food bank was starting to get a little traffic since many knew what was coming and they began to plan for no paycheck.

Attendance at the sites was solid all week and the picketers remained steadfast and upbeat. I kept my routine of regularly visiting all the picket sites in Seattle, Renton, Kent and Auburn. The major sites had good visibility since they were located on highly trafficked roads. Everybody knew we were on strike. No authority compelled people to come out to the line for their picket shift. In most industrial unions a picketer receives strike pay for meeting their picket shift requirements. Since we had no strike pay there was no incentive to show up for the assigned picket line shift except the incentive to win this strike. The number of Boeing employees on strike is widely reported between 16 and 18 thousand. Nobody had an exact count and if Boeing knew, they weren't saying.

I was always surprised at how well the sites were attended and on the line in Kent, where I worked, I recognized many of my co-workers. I was impressed by some of the real star engineering talents I saw carrying picket signs. Not everybody hung around the picket sites as I was to learn. Some got part-time jobs, others went skiing, and others took care of long-neglected home maintenance but everybody supported the strike — except those who didn't. We saw a few each day in the morning cross the line and go to work. I have no idea what it was like to sit alone in a cubical in those empty offices and do what?

A cold dark night

I had heard we needed some support at one of the "flying squad" sites at one of the warehouse areas. I got the address and it was dark by the time I got there. This was one of the picket sites that sprang up to slow down Boeing freight deliveries. The picket site was dark and down a side street with nothing but dark warehouses for blocks. That night the weather had started turning colder. The guys had managed to scrounge up one of the illegal open barrels and had a fire going. Since there was absolutely no one around it didn't seem to matter. I was sure that the EPA inspector wasn't cruising these back streets in the industrial warehouse district looking for violations.

There were about eight of us including me. I didn't know any of them but as the night wore on we exchanged stories. It turned out one of them was on the engineering negotiation team at the last contract negotiations with Boeing before the McDonnell Douglas merger. We all talked about the changes in the corporate culture that have evolved since then. It was generally recognized that this culture change was a big factor in the current strike. When we compared the differences in the two negotiations up to this point we believed it really was part of the overall plan to marginalize the influence of the engineering community.

There was a light rain later that night and it was definitely getting colder. I was starting to feel it and the cold added to the rain made me feel miserable. So I did what everybody does in those circumstances. You throw another chunk of wood in the burn barrel and stand closer. We did see at least one truck come down the street and when the driver saw our picket signs, he stopped and turned around. We watched the tail lights fade away. The guys had been here the night before and since it was already midnight the discussion was how long should we keep the picket line up. These "Flying Squad" sites were not permanent since Boeing would constantly relocate freight drop-offs. I knew I wasn't going to leave until we all decided we've done all we could that night.

After a few more hours the guys who worked the site the previous night thought we should wrap it up and I didn't argue with them. I got to know those guys that night and when they talked about where they worked and what their jobs were, I realized they weren't on strike for more money. These guys were high on the pay scale and held important positions but not management positions. In the old Boeing these engineers would be seen as colleagues by management and their opinions were sought out and they were treated with respect. Now clearly they were employees and their job responsibilities were narrowly defined. The realization that there was no recognition of the experience and sound judgment they brought to the job was evident in the new Boeing workplace. Engineers were interchangeable like cogs in a machine. This was an attack on their professionalism so they stood out in the cold dark rain and seethed.

There was no doubt in my mind from then on that this strike was about a lot more than money. Certainly, there were many strikers in lower-paying jobs and the benefit erosions in the rejected contract offers made their positions worse. I had many conversations on the picket line with people whom I knew who were in lower-paying jobs. But they would almost always only talk about the lack of respect in those lousy contract offers.

When I finally got home I was still numb from being wet and cold. I decided I had to up my game if I was going to last. In the morning after I checked in at headquarters, I swung over to the mall a couple of miles away. I went to the big sporting goods store and I was in luck since it was already mid-February all the ski parkas were 50% off and there was a sign on the rack stating take another 40% off today! I found a great bright red down-filled parka that was waterproof and had some reflective strips on it for visibility at night. This was perfect and I was ready for the worst. I stopped by home for lunch before heading back to the picket lines. I had a chance to read the morning paper and catch the local news on TV at noon. The latest news was that Boeing still had not delivered any airplanes and since it was Wednesday the SPEEA strike had now lasted a full week. It was also reported that Boeing stock was down 22%. A Boeing spokesperson claimed that management can fill in for the striking workers. If that were true that means the company has an extra 18,000 employees they don't need. They also had a clip of Phil stating that the company was prepared for a long strike. Jeez Phil, really? My first thought when I heard that was, "Is next year good for you Phil? Because that works for me."

We were having regular strategy meetings and a big concern was not to come off as a bunch of whiny over-paid Boeing employees. This was a genuine concern since our average take-home pay was significantly higher than the average pay in the area. Our union messaging was never about we're striking for higher pay. The leadership had no way to impose any "gag order" on the "rank and file", but when the media would interview picketers on the line the message was always the same: "We're out here fighting for fair treatment and respect."

I had to go back to Auburn toward the end of the week. I got a call that another back gate was opening up and the picketers were going to set up a line. It was already dark and I asked Betty if she wanted to check out the Auburn sites. She was going out to the sites regularly but not every day, all day with me. She said let's go nothing's going on here tonight. When we got there I knew some of the picketers and we set up the stove and started a fire. The back gate wasn't nearly as fun as the big site at the main gate, It was quieter and darker but there was spillover light from the plant so it wasn't too bad. I knew one of the woman engineers and we spent an hour or two discussing where we were and what the next few weeks looked like.

Since some of these picket sites were isolated, safety was a concern from the start of the strike. Nobody thought it was reasonable to expect individuals to stand by themselves at 2 a.m. in the dark, especially women. Hell, I'm a middle-aged bald guy and I wouldn't want to stand out there alone in the middle of the night. We advised all our picketers to just keep going and don't stop if they showed up at a site and it didn't look safe.

It was getting close to shift change for the third shift and once again it was starting to get cold and a light rain was falling. We had been out at this gate for about four hours. I was fairly warm and dry in my new parka but Betty was beginning to look like a drowned cat. About that time a newer pickup truck pulled up and stopped in front of us just outside the gate. The driver rolled down the window and handed over a huge bag of McDonald's Big Macs. He said it was just something he wanted to do to cheer us up and show support. We thanked him enthusiastically and he disappeared through the gate. I looked over at Betty and she had her burger unwrapped and clutched in her hands. She said "This is the best burger I ever ate." Yes it was, we all thought so.

Seeing Betty rain-soaked standing at a picket site in the middle of the night reminded me of a few nights ago when we were at the Renton Field picket site. It was again near midnight and light rain was falling. I was talking with a few of the picketers and Betty came over and caught my eye. She told me I should go over and talk with them and gestured towards two guys over on the other side of the stove since they are complaining they are standing out here in the wet and cold at midnight while the negotiators are home and warm in their beds.

I did just that and introduced myself as one of the negotiation team. They were a little taken aback, but we quickly became caught up in a worthwhile discussion which probably went on for an hour. While I was driving home I realized just how important it was to stay connected because if we let a gap develop between the rank and file and the union leadership, this strike will fall apart. When I left those two guys they were smiling and we shook hands and they told me to keep up the good fight and we're all in this together.

The second week was over but there were two events announced in "Line on the Line" for the weekend. Saturday there was to be a "Union Solidarity Day" at the Frederickson site which was the southernmost Boeing plant in Puget Sound. Sunday there would be a free pancake breakfast for all the strikers at the Tukwila Community Hall. Betty and I went to both. It was great fun and I got to talk with a lot of my fellow strikers, some of whom I hadn't seen since the day we walked out. From everything I could see we were solid going into our third week on the line. The attitude of everyone I talked with was positive and they were determined to stay out as long as it takes.

CHAPTER 5

THIRD WEEK

I got up early Monday morning because I wanted to catch the local news on TV before I went out to the picket lines. We were starting our third week of the strike and I wanted to see how the local TV stations covered it. Ever since the strike started King 5, the NBC affiliate, has been opening every local news show with picket line video and a subtitle showing the duration of the strike. What had changed this morning was that the first thing the news anchor said was, "When will this strike end?" The tide was definitely turning. We were no longer being portrayed as the "ne'er-do-well" wannabe strikers.

I put two stoves and some spare parts and tools in the truck and I stopped to pick up Morris on the way to the Kent site. We had worked for more than a week on converting the open barrels to the enclosed stoves. Now we would routinely check the sites and see if we missed something. We also became the maintenance crew and if something was loose or fell off a stove we made repairs on the spot.

By now most of the picketers were settling into their picket routine and seemed to be resolved to stick it out. I was talking with some of the picketers and we were all in agreement, we were here for the duration. Nobody had a good idea of what that duration would be, but some were already saying another month wouldn't be a problem at all.

Feeding the picketers

As I was walking up and down the line with my sign I came across one of the senior engineers I knew. Hal's job, when he was working at Boeing, was to help design a booster rocket that would be launched from the Space Shuttle to send satellites into high earth orbit. Hal really was a rocket scientist and now he was committed to walking the picket line with the same enthusiasm he brought to rocket science.

Hal lived on Vashon Island and he would get up early to bake blueberry muffins with his wife. Then he would pack up a dozen or so and have enough time to catch the ferry he would normally take into work at the Boeing Space Center. Instead of going to work he would deliver fresh muffins to the picket line. He would picket for the morning shift and then go back home. This was Hal's routine during the strike and he told me he would keep it up as long as it takes.

If morale at the Kent picket site is typical then going into the third week shows no sign of any loss of commitment to our goals. The donations to the Strike Fund have been steadily growing. We have close to $100,000 in donations. The first zero paycheck is a week away and that realization is increasing the pressure on the picketers. Food donations have been growing although traffic at the food bank is low. Next week will be hard and I expect hardship cases to increase. We are getting more support from other unions and the community at large. We regularly get more and more drop-offs of donuts, pizza, burgers and coffee. One morning there was one of the big Starbucks' take out coffee boxes, a box of sweeteners, creamers and a stack of cups. A number of the local eateries that cater to the Boeing lunch crowds are offering specials, discounts and even free food for the strikers.

Food was steadily becoming a regular part of our picket sites which surprised me. I had never thought about this during the strike planning. I don't remember anyone from the other unions or the labor council saying anything about this at all. I think this is unique to our strike and grew organically out of the self-organizing approach. It was simple, we had a lot of people on the line, and they came and went

24 hours a day. If you want them to stay longer, figure out how to feed them. We even had lots of children visit the line. Nobody wanted the children to go hungry. This was not a perfect solution and there was a lot of junk food but I did see a lot of kids running around with a donut in their hand.

Back to the line

Later that morning I checked back at headquarters and got a message that the negotiating team would have a meeting tomorrow. We have been having regular meetings since we went out but this one was flagged important. The consensus at headquarters was that going into the third week all the regular picket sites were well-attended. A few isolated sites spring up and disappear as required. Boeing is still having problems getting freight delivered.

We regularly stop rail cars delivering to Fredrickson, Renton and Everett but that is only a temporary delay. The train crew will not cross our picket line, so they stop the train and call it into the dispatcher. The train sits until the rail company sends out a manager driver who moves the train onto Boeing property. This results in a few hours of delay. When truck freight refuses to cross the line, the truck usually keeps on its route and returns the freight to the warehouse. That is why the company is regularly setting up alternate drop-offs.

Morris and I spent the rest of the day visiting as many of the sites as we could from Boeing Headquarters and Boeing Field and then south through Renton, Kent and finally Auburn. Each of these locations had multiple gates. Since there were at least two dozen picket sites we couldn't stop at every one, there just weren't enough hours in the day. We would drive past every gate at the location. If we saw something that looked like it needed attention or some of the picketers waved us over we would pull over and park. We would share the latest information and spend some time reviewing what was the latest news and usually get something to eat. It was easy to spend an hour every time we stopped.

The next morning I went to headquarters for an early negotiating team meeting. I found out that Richard Barnes was coming back to mediate another bargaining session between us and the Boeing company. In some ways this was surprising since the company message has been there would not be any changes to the second offer which had been rejected. Barnes had told us when he left he would come back when we asked him. I wasn't aware the union asked him, it didn't come up in any of the strategy meetings I was at. I went to every negotiation team meeting that was scheduled but I didn't know what triggered this change.

What I did find out was that Barnes had been routinely calling Boeing to get them back to the table. Since they had withdrawn the last offer we had nothing to vote on. It was very clear to Barnes we were not going to end the strike and go back to work without a contract — at least not in the foreseeable future anyway. Our information was that Boeing had missed 12 deliveries by now and airline support had dwindled to a trickle. The information from all our contacts inside the Boeing buildings confirmed the strike was having a big impact in many areas. Activity on the production line has slowed way down and the engineering areas looked like ghost towns.

We decided to review our last proposal and be ready to have something to bring to the table. We set up some meetings to do this and the staff experts got to work to prepare our proposal. We really were not even close to giving up the farm but we did want to do an honest review and it was especially important to honor the commitment of the thousands of picketers that were standing out on the line. There was no confusion about that.

The big march

While I was there I also learned of a big rally and march that was planned for tomorrow. Flyers for the rally had been printed and were at all the picket sites. We were getting a huge amount of support from the Teamsters and the Machinists on this. The rally was to be a mass march from the Machinists' union hall in South Park and end up in front of Boeing headquarters just over a mile away. The Teamsters had a 40 foot truck that had sides that would open up to create a stage. The truck was painted in the Teamster colors and emblems. It was so clean and shiny it sparkled in the sunlight. The Boeing headquarters across from Boeing Field had a big public area in front of it and a big cutout off the 4-lane East Marginal Way for busses. The plan was to have the Teamster truck show up in that spot just before the marchers arrived. On the stage was a rock and roll band and they were ready to rock.

There was a big crowd at the Machinists' hall parking lot at 1:30 p.m. ready to march. We had pipers leading the march and luckily for us it was a beautiful afternoon. The news media gave the crowd size at about 2,500. As we filed out of the parking lot I noticed one of the local TV news helicopters hovering above. We had definitely become the news story that everyone was following. We soon overflowed the sidewalk and we were taking up a full lane of the street. The local police were out diverting traffic and we even had a lead car with the blue lights flashing. The spirit was infectious, even the cops were smiling.

Part of the route crossed over the Duwamish river

via a moderately high bridge. As we all hiked uphill to the top of the bridge we got a pretty good view. This was an industrial area, so we got a great view of the river winding through warehouses and the back of the old Boeing building where they made B-17 Bombers in World War II. As I got to the top I looked over towards Boeing Field and laughed out loud. In the clear blue sky, a small single-engine plane was towing a long banner: **"WHATEVER IT TAKES — AS LONG AS IT TAKES! SPEEA"** I was near the front and when I looked back from my vantage point I couldn't see the end of the line. I think some were still in the parking lot over a half-mile away.

As we marched downhill we picked up some momentum. We were getting near Boeing headquarters and the marchers were getting very enthusiastic. We came around the corner and in two blocks we were there. The big blue Teamster truck was right there and as soon as they saw us coming around the corner the band sprang to life. They had a pretty good cover of Aretha's "Respect." When we all finally got in front of Boeing headquarters there were a few speakers but that program was short. The whole rally quickly became a rock and roll festival and some of us were dancing in the street.

We had been on the picket lines for exactly two full weeks and at least with this crowd, there were no signs of letting up. There were no signs on the picket lines that the commitment to carry out the strike was wavering in any way. If anything it seemed that the number of people was growing at each site at least during the day. It was naturally a little skimpier at night between midnight and 6 a.m. but when I would stop at the major sites we would have a half dozen or more picketers.

Our block party at Boeing headquarters lasted about two hours and by that time it was time to get home and feed the kids. I don't know who organized the rally and march. I did see some people I recognized from other unions who had been helping us with the strike planning and I'm sure they organized this event. The news gave us good coverage and it was a big morale booster for the people who were there and those who weren't.

Back to the table again

Thursday, February 24 the strike was officially in the third week. We were notified by Boeing that they were, at the request of the Federal Mediator, willing to meet with us for a bargaining session. Barnes had routinely called us to assess our willingness to return to the negotiation table with Boeing. Our answer was always yes because for the union we need a contract to end the strike. Boeing was not as willing to go back to the table. If they wait long enough and the strike collapses then everybody goes back to work. They don't need a union contract if everybody is at work, which pretty much solves the problem for them.

It was becoming increasingly obvious that we were not likely to be back in the near future and Boeing's production problems were getting worse. Everyone knew that the Engineers rejected the second offer by only a 51% majority. I'm sure Boeing thought this was a chance to tweak the last offer enough and considering the economic pressure on the strikers, it wouldn't take much to flip those numbers in another vote.

The news of renewed talks between SPEEA and Boeing was picked up and reported by the local press and media the day before the scheduled meeting. This was the only thing people were talking about when I stopped at picket sites that day. The advice I got from the strikers was "Don't cave in" and "Stay strong, we can win this." We had done everything possible to prepare ourselves and the strikers on the line, it was time to sit across the table again with Boeing.

We didn't see the Boeing negotiators when we first got to the hotel conference center across from Sea-Tac airport. A large conference room was booked jointly by the union and the company and we each had reserved meeting rooms isolated from each other. We were not going to be mingling in the hallways or have any interactions outside that conference room without Richard Barnes, the federal mediator, present. We had been asked by Barnes to remain in our meeting room until he could meet with us.

While we were waiting for Barnes there was not much to do, we had already reviewed everything we had twice and we were reviewing our options depending on what the company would offer. We did assume there would be another offer since it made no sense at all for them to agree to this negotiation session and then tell us and Barnes they were not changing their last offer.

Barnes knocked on our conference room door and asked if we could meet with him now. Barnes was very respectful towards us and was always courteous but he was clear with us that he was running these negotiations. When he came into the room we all assembled at the large conference table and he sat at the head. He started off by acknowledging that we had surprised everyone with our tenacity and resolve in conducting this strike. He then turned to our responsibilities to the thousands of families that are going without a paycheck and the financial hardship that was increasing each day the strike continued.

He again reminded us that the mandate of the FMCS was to resolve labor disputes. He said he needed to understand the current situation and then try to find a way to end this strike. He asked us what our issues were with the last Boeing offer and we responded that the last offer still fell far short of our member's expectations and we certainly didn't think these expectations were unreasonable. We told him we were convinced that the company simply wanted to impose their contract and had never bargained in good faith. We had a good discussion with Barnes, he would ask us specific questions and we would respond, he was affable and candid with us.

We spent a couple of hours with Barnes that first meeting. He finally said he had a clear understanding of our position and now he will meet with Boeing. He told us he will not bring the two sides together until he feels face-to-face talks would be worthwhile. We were left to ourselves until later that afternoon. Barnes again came to our conference room door and asked to meet with us.

We got to go home early that first night because we had nothing new to look at and had reviewed every possible outcome. The next morning we had a brief meeting but of course, nothing new happened overnight that we knew of. Barnes came to the door and said he would like to discuss the results of yesterday's meeting with Boeing. He told us Boeing had a new offer they would like to present and he reviewed his guidelines for the meeting. If he knew any of the offer details he did not share them with us. He said that we would be given the opportunity to respond. He also strongly requested that for the duration of the talks we make no public comments. He said he will ask for the same agreement from Boeing.

After some informal discussion of the process and expectations, Barnes said he was going to meet with Boeing to determine if they are ready to make a presentation. It was already mid-morning and he said that we can expect to meet with the company after lunch. We would be notified when that will happen. We finally had something new to discuss. It was clear that we would see a third offer but we had no idea what it would look like. We thought maybe the company was going to blink first and we would get some meaningful concessions.

After lunch, we were back in our meeting room and Barnes came to our door. He told us the company had a presentation for us and he expected us to listen and in the end, we would get another contract proposal. At that time we would be given copies to review but there would be no discussion or counter-proposals by us until the following day. We headed for the big conference room and it was empty. We took our seats on one side of the long table and we were followed in by Barnes who sat at the head.

Presently the company filed in. There were not as many people as we were used to seeing. We had the same negotiators and support staff we had in all the previous meetings but the company team was barely half the size. They filed in without making eye contact and what struck me was the absolute silence. Their lowest ranking member sat across from me again. He did give me a slight nod and we made eye contact. I am only guessing but I definitely got the impression he was saying, yes this sucks, but there's nothing I can do about it.

Well, there were brief opening remarks by their chief negotiator in which he basically stated after careful thought and consideration, the company was prepared to make this best and final offer to the union. We had heard that statement "best and final offer" twice before and we didn't believe this time either. The other thing we had heard repeatedly was "There will be no additional money." We didn't believe that either and it turned out we were right.

The company launched into the major parts of the offer. The key economic features of salary pools, medical plans, and retirement were presented. It was immediately clear that this offer was almost identical to the offer that was almost universally rejected back in December. The two most notable changes were a half percent increase to the engineering salary pools and a stock option of 100 shares awarded over a 5-year period. The presentation was high level and proceeded without interruption. We didn't have an opportunity to question or counter any part of the offer at that time. Copies of the proposed contract were passed out and Barnes adjourned the meeting. Boeing was in and out in less than 30 minutes. Barnes stayed behind and told us we now needed to take the time to carefully review the proposal. He did advise us that in his experience this was a big concession from Boeing and there were not likely to be any further meetings or improvement. Barnes said that he scheduled a joint meeting tomorrow where we could make any counter-proposals.

Back in our meeting room, we spent the rest of the afternoon going over the company's proposal with a fine-tooth comb. The offer was almost identical to the original offer except for a very small amount of additional money. The provisions for medical premiums and higher deductibles were delayed for a year. The changes to the pension plan were still there and the retiree medical benefits were eliminated for the new hires. The standard monthly pension benefit was bumped up by $4 per year. Aside from these very modest changes the only other difference from the first offer was the addition of the stock option of 100 shares. It was Friday night and we were tired and hungry. We decided to reconvene in the morning and prepare our response.

Driving back to the hotel Saturday morning I came to the conclusion that I didn't want to take that offer out to the members for a vote. I still had a bad taste in my mouth from the last time. I picked up a large coffee at the kiosk in the lobby and went to our meeting room. We double-checked the proposal again to see if we missed anything and put it aside. The consensus was that this was unacceptable and we began to rework our last counter-proposal to counter the company's offer. After a few hours, we had what we wanted and by then Barnes had come over to our room and told us he scheduled a session with the company after lunch.

We finally had the discussion of exactly what we would do if Boeing would not consider our counter. After some careful thought we all agreed, we were not going to take that offer out for a vote. The strikers on the line have been clear about what it would take to end the strike and this was not it.

We were called back to the main conference room after lunch, this time the company negotiators were seated and waiting for us. When we were seated their chief negotiator asked us if we had any questions. We then reviewed the major features of the offer and said we had a counter-proposal. We had the same issues that we had the last two times. The company's responses were terse and it was obvious that their negotiator was becoming visibly agitated. There was no cooperative atmosphere and once again it was clear this was "take it or leave it." It certainly seemed that they were there only to show good faith bargaining in front of the federal mediator. After a few heated exchanges what followed were only more heated exchanges. The meeting was over, Barnes saw that bargaining if you can call it that, had ended.

We finally said since this offer did not meet any of our needs we would leave it on the table and not bring it out to the members for a vote. That statement visibly shook them and I think that decision was totally unexpected. In short, most of the company's side were pissed and the spokesman told Barnes there was nothing left to discuss. Barnes looked resigned and declared the session over.

We were all filing out of the room and there was some muttering and comments but we were all leaving together. Then I saw something which surprised me but showed just how tense things had become.

The big double doors of the room opened and in the hall were TV news cameras and lights. I was still back at the table picking up some papers and I saw Linda our only woman engineer negotiator just about ready to step through the door. Approaching her quickly from behind was one of the company's team. I saw him raise his arm without breaking stride to shove Linda out of the way. I think I saw his palm just touch her coat before he stopped short in his tracks. This is how bad it had gotten and how close Linda came to being shoved out of the way on live TV by a Boeing manager. Judging how fast that guy was moving she probably would have landed on her face.

We packed up and got out of there. Back at the SPEEA office we put together a news release and got the word out to the line. When I got home I told the whole story to Betty and she said "Nice try but the strike ain't over yet." I went down to the Kent picket sites after I ate to help get the news out. Since everyone was waiting for news about the third negotiations I had a crowd engaged for several hours as strikers came and went. More than one person said we did the right thing by leaving that offer on the table. About midnight a reporter joined the group and interviewed me and some of the picketers. He ran a story the next day about the failed negotiations and his observation that the picketers were not discouraged and resolved to keep the strike going.

Sunday morning I went to the picket sites in Kent, Auburn and Renton to give everybody I could the information on the negotiations that ended Saturday night. As the news settled in and people thought about it the overwhelming agreement was "This strike ain't over yet."

About mid-afternoon I went back to the picket site at Boeing headquarters to see Vice President Al Gore visit our picketers. This was a big deal and there was a large boisterous crowd to greet him. He stayed for an hour or so and it did boost our morale. We were definitely having an impact with our strike.

CHAPTER 6

FOURTH WEEK

I was out on the picket lines early Monday morning. After the collapse of the negotiations Saturday night the strikers wanted information, they wanted to know what was going on. I wasn't sure what to expect but very soon I found out that people were going to dig in and hunker down. Everyone I talked with said we did the right thing to leave the offer on the table. One person said, "We already voted no to all those takeaways, what part of no don't they understand?"

There was no wavering in the resolve to win this strike that I could see. In fact, the commitment to continue the strike just kept on growing. One example in Kent surprised me. We always had a big turnout at the Kent site but parking was always a problem. We wouldn't park on company property as a matter of pride. Even though there was ample parking outside the security gates you would still have to cross the picket line to get there. No striker was going to cross the line. So cars parked for blocks around the picket sites.

There was a big grassy field across from the Kent back gate that offered ample parking a short walk from the lines. The problem was that after three weeks of cars pulling in and out maneuvering into parking spots, the strip along the street was turning into a mud bog. When I drove over there this morning there was a long fresh strip of gravel completely covering the mud. I asked some of the regulars at the site what was up with that. The response I got was that last week a few of them got tired of dealing with the crappy parking so they took up a collection and paid for a truckload of gravel. When it was delivered the driver immediately sized up the situation, raised the truck bed and smoothly spread out the gravel. Fifteen minutes later we had first-class off-site picket parking. The picketer's comment was "If we're going to be here for a while, we might as well make a few improvements." I heard later that over at the Renton Field site some picketers talked about spreading some grass seed in a few muddy areas but held off when one pointed out that then they would need to mow it when the weather warmed up.

This was going to be a hard week for us. Thursday is payday and no one will see a paycheck. This will be the first zero check since the strike started. The financial pressure is building but people are becoming very resilient and finding ways to cope with the loss of income. With 18,000 people not getting a paycheck, this has had a big impact on many. Some people are starting to struggle but others like myself had some savings to fall back on. I was having a conversation with one younger engineer who told me when he walked out on day one he had three credit cards that were completely maxed out. He was actually quite optimistic about the future and reflected that up until now he didn't give much thought to what his plans were. He said he felt he was in robot mode: all he did was go to work, buy stuff he really didn't need, wait for payday, send money to the credit card companies and then repeat. He summed up the strike so far as a positive experience for him, "It's giving me a chance to think about what I really want and what matters to me." For all of us, this was a "Time Out" from our regular lives for sure. I talked to many picketers who had the same thoughts.

People on the line were almost universally in good spirits. It turned out it was pleasant to hang out with friends and make some new ones. There was a ready bond of shared experiences. It was usually busy during the day, there always seemed to be some activity going on and picketers were always coming and going. At night it got quieter but it could still be pleasant. Even with a steady gentle rain, talking quietly with friends was relaxing. Having the time to think about important things without having to kept track of the time was very therapeutic. When I walked around the lines any hour of day or night I always got a pleasant nod and more often than not, a smile.

A visit from the AFL-CIO

It was the last day of February and we got an extra day thanks to leap year. I stopped by SPEEA headquarters for a negotiation team meeting, and among other things, we planned for a visit from John Sweeney, the President of AFL-CIO, to some of our picket sites later today. This was a big morale booster since we were getting more press coverage every day the strike lasted. We were planning to have a meeting in the big theater at the Southcenter Mall the next day and we needed to prepare for it. We had a summary of the last offer and a review of our current activities and the status of all the picket lines. We felt we were prepared to answer strikers' questions.

After the meeting, I found out when Sweeney would be at the Renton picket sites so I went over to Renton. When I got there Sweeney was on the back of a flatbed truck speaking to a large crowd of enthusiastic picketers. He pledged the continuing support of all organized labor and was well-received and made a big impression on the crowd. He stuck around a while talking with the strikers and answering questions. I got a chance to spend some time with him and we talked about the negotiations and strike support. He was very impressed with what SPEEA had accomplished. He admitted that he was somewhat skeptical when he first learned of our intention to strike. He knew we had never carried out any serious strike in our history. He said our determination and resourcefulness really were an inspiration to all organized labor.

I stuck around the Renton sites until it started getting dark and then I went south to the Kent sites. There were all new picketers by then so the discussions of the weekend events and Sweeney's visit were still hot topics. News had spread about the big meeting in Southcenter tomorrow and many were planning to attend.

Boeing declares impasse — Is the strike over?

Wednesday, March 1 was another milestone since the strike was now on day 21 or three full weeks on the line. This was, of course, reported on the morning news but there was a new wrinkle in the strike story. Boeing notified us and issued a statement to the media that they had declared the negotiations were at an impasse and they would begin implementing provisions of the last contract offer. They also announced that they would begin distributing the salary increases specified by the new contract.

This announcement caused a huge uproar on the lines. Many strikers didn't understand what implementing the contract meant. Some people thought the strike was over and went back to work. We immediately had our legal counsel prepare a letter that was distributed to all the picket sites explaining the strike was not over and their rights as strikers were still fully protected. We heard the next day of a few that crossed the lines but then came back out and were joined by a few more new strikers.

Lines were already forming when I got to the big Southcenter theater. This was a huge auditorium and we must have had a thousand people there and it was standing room only by the time we started. We covered the last negotiation session and the success we'd had so far in maintaining the picket sites. We had a microphone set up in the aisle so people could come up and get their questions answered. We also gave our best assessment of what effect the strike was having on company operations. We also heard from the strikers, the reports they were getting from relatives who were still at work at jobs not represented by SPEEA. The reports were all the same: the production areas, engineering offices, and test labs were virtual ghost towns.

The meeting never got rowdy but the attendees were definitely loud and boisterous. The enthusiasm for the strike was still there which surprised me. I would have thought the strikers would be a little more somber since we would soon be in the second month of the strike. Of course, I only saw people who supported the strike and that affected my perspective. The media was on our side because their stories never talked about shrinking picket sites or mass defections to cross the line. We had absolutely gained the support of the community and the donations to the strike fund and the union food bank kept growing.

When the meeting broke up after a few hours people still lingered in the parking lot, mostly small groups of co-workers comparing notes and catching up. I ran into a few people I hadn't seen since the strike began and did the same thing. The one important thing I learned that day was nobody was considering going back to work. Many thought Boeing's announcement was an attempt to demoralize us. If that were so, it totally failed. If anything, the effect of the promised raises if we returned to work only stiffened our resolve. That's the day I started seeing small handwritten signs, "As long as it takes." If that's what it's going to be, we've already cut our teeth on the line — bring it on. I went back to the picket lines until late that night and the same conversations continued, all with the same outcome, we were hunkering down for the next month.

The next day I was back on the line early and the morning shift was still talking about yesterday's developments. One thing we all had in common and didn't talk about was payday. This was the first payday that no striker would be getting a paycheck. Going into the fourth week of the strike we were all developing strategies to deal with the lack of cash flow. But it was getting a lot harder for some than others. I remember when I started at Boeing, I had no cash reserves, we pretty much lived paycheck to paycheck. Every payday Betty and I would go out that weekend and buy enough groceries to feed the kids for two weeks. We had to make sure we had enough money set aside to buy gas to get to work and pay the rent at the end of the month. We were lucky, we always had enough. If there was a strike I'm not sure how we would have survived. I now know food would not have been an issue. There was one hole card that some played. Boeing had a 401k savings plan. You could borrow against it by going online and requesting a loan. Some of that money was Boeing money and strikers borrowed it to stay on strike.

Restocking the pantry

About mid-morning I went up to the SPEEA office to check-in and I saw a semi-truck and trailer in the parking lot. It turns out we had just gotten a delivery of 20,000 lbs of onions for the food bank and all hands were needed to unload it. So for the next hour, I joined in and carried bags of onions into the food bank we had set up in one conference room.

We were working too hard to talk much while unloading because we had been asked to get the truck unloaded ASAP so the driver could get going. When we were done we had bags of onions stacked to the ceiling in every nook and corner we could find.

I had to find out how we got all these onions and it was a great story. It turns out that there was a warehouse in central Oregon with a load of unsold onions that was abandoned by the grower. The dispatcher at the warehouse who happened to be a Teamster and had been following our strike was asked by his boss if he knew anybody that would remove the onions.

The dispatcher called our office number and asked if we want 20,000 lbs of onions for our food bank. The receptionist said, "Yes we do, let me get someone on the line to get the details." So one of the food bank volunteers got on the line and the dispatcher said if we wanted these onions could we send a truck down and pick them up. Well, he was told, "That would be hard for us since we're not truckers." He said, "Let me get back to you maybe I can get a trucker to bring them up to you."

We got a call back a little later and he said he found a driver deadheading an empty trailer from California to Seattle who would be willing to swing by the warehouse and pick up the onions for us. So that is exactly what happened. When that Teamster brother showed up, the warehouse crew loaded the onions. Whether they were on the clock or not didn't really matter to the boss, since he was likely a former Teamster in his younger days, he just wanted the onions gone.

We thanked the driver and told him we were very grateful and these would be put to good use. He was very gracious and said he was more than happy to help some strikers trying to get a fair contract.

Getting rid of 20,000 lbs of onions wasn't easy. We immediately started shipping bags to our Everett office food bank since we had a lot of vehicles going back and forth. We started breaking down the big bags into smaller 5 lb paper sacks for our food bank clients. Someone came up with the idea to find a good recipe for onion soup and put a copy in all the bags. So that's what we did and I took dozens of bags to the picket lines for days and handed out as many as I could.

The number of people showing up at the food banks was increasing noticeably since we had been out for almost a month. The pace of donations was exceeding the demand and we were slowly storing more and more food. I had stopped by the office with Betty and saw the family groups coming out with bags of groceries and I said I wanted to get a bag. Betty objected and thought we should leave the food for the people that needed it. I told her the food's not going to run out since we can't move it out faster than it's coming in and besides I want to eat the same food that some of the other strikers are eating.

After a month there was no slacking in the support from the community. Food donations kept on coming. From collecting, sorting and eating the food donations I saw four ways that people would share food. It started with people just bringing food to the picket line and handing it out. Although this was usually what we'd call "junk" food, but not always, it was appreciated and disappeared quickly. The second was people who sorted through their cabinets and donated their surplus cans and boxes, sometimes they were a little dusty but all were usable. The third approach was simply to go to the market or Costco and buy an 8-pack of canned chili or other useful non-perishable food items, box them up and drop them off. Lastly just like the free pancake breakfast 2 weeks ago there were still sponsored events by other unions and local businesses to feed the strikers.

As the weekend approached the turmoil of Boeing's impasse declaration was dying down and we had filed another Unfair Labor Practice (ULP) complaint with the National Labor Relations Board (NLRB). None of these were going to have an immediate effect on the strike but it was important to protect our legal rights. An important right was that an employee could not be fired while participating in a legal strike.

Medical coverage at risk

The beginning of March brought more pressure on the strikers, the media carried stories that the health insurance for all the strikers expired on the first of March. This is actually a murky issue and Boeing was not going to explain options or clarify the issues for the strikers. In fact, Boeing does not have any insurance. Boeing is self-insured, so although the benefits are administered by various insurance companies, Boeing simply writes a check each month to cover the medical costs and administration fees. To qualify for plan benefits you had to be an employee. Employees that are on strike are still employees.

This was a very scary issue for many strikers. SPEEA had prepared information on the temporary COBRA coverage which is available for employees who have lost their employer's coverage. By a quirk in the rules, a person can apply up to 60 days after receiving treatment for reimbursement. I talked with one engineer whose wife was undergoing chemotherapy. The potential loss of his medical insurance coverage was terrifying to him because of the huge costs of his wife's care. I couldn't tell him what he should do but what I did say was that if he chose to cross the line and return to work, I would completely understand.

As it turned out Boeing did not cancel everybody's medical plan coverage. They were silent on the issue. Based on media accounts we found out some providers decided Boeing strikers had no coverage and must pay at the time of service. Other providers simply continued business as usual and submitted the charges to Boeing. There is no doubt this created even more anxiety for the strikers. Even with the lack of regular paychecks and growing uncertainty about when and how the strike would end, the determination to prevail was still as strong as ever. Strikers were still holding signs on the picket lines proclaiming, "As long as it takes."

At the end of the strike, Boeing announced that if any striking employee paid out of pocket medical expenses those claims would be accepted and paid at the plan reimbursement rates. The result was the strikers' medical coverage was actually continued throughout the strike although there was no way of knowing this at the time. This was a huge relief to some of the strikers and softened the company's image when it was time to go back to work.

Keeping the line going

As we ended the fourth week we had some milder weather and the sites were all active and well attended. The strikers were engaged and pro-active. About mid-morning in front of the Space Center in Kent, I saw a small group gathering at one end of our site and I could hear faint Bluegrass music. I walked over with some others and I saw a traditional Bluegrass band with a crowd gathered around. Out of the 18,000 employees out on strike I wasn't surprised, there were lots of good musicians. These guys were very good and played quite a few of the standard Bluegrass songs. The picketers were really enjoying the music. Bluegrass (along with classic Rock and Roll as we already know) turns out to be a perfect music genre for a picket line. Upbeat and up-tempo works perfectly.

I talked with the guys when they were done. It turns out they have been playing together for a few years and tried to attend the local festivals as much as possible. They said they had been out a few times now as long as it's not raining. They wanted to demonstrate they're not ready to quit anytime soon and said it's fun to come out and play for fellow picketers.

I checked back at headquarters later and the receptionist said that Maria was looking for me. I found Maria and she told me we had a burn barrel problem at the south end of Boeing Field. I had thought those problems were all behind us by now. I still kept tools and spare parts in the back of the truck that Morris and I would occasionally need to make a few repairs. These stoves have been burning continuously for over three weeks and much of that time they were glowing red. Although there were no open 55 gallon drums still in use, the common term was still burn barrel. I preferred calling them the SPEEA stove, but I did start to hear SPEEA burn barrel which I thought was just fine.

Maria told me we got a call from Seattle's code enforcement about an irritating smoke complaint from a business next to a picket site. He said if we don't take care of it, he will cite us and we can expect a fine. I told Maria I'm on my way. It was a clear afternoon and when I got close to the site I saw dark smoke billowing around the site. Rats I thought, what the hell is going on?

After I parked, walking over to the burn barrel I saw the problem. There was some good dry firewood piled nearby but there was also a heap of debris that looked like somebody tore down their chicken coop and dropped it off. The picket captain recognized me and came over for the latest news. I told him we got a complaint from Seattle about the smoke. I pointed to what was left of the chicken coop and said we can't be burning that junk. The reason we have all that smoke is the fire isn't nearly hot enough to burn that half-rotten wood. We hadn't had any problems with smoke since we got the SPEEA burn barrels on line. I figured out that due to the few days of mild weather nobody really needed the hot fire, so the stove was left to smolder.

I started to restack the dry wood neatly near the burn barrel and threw in some of the smaller pieces to get the fire blazing. Within a few minutes, the smoke was gone. This was what I had in mind when I designed this thing. With any kind of reasonable fire, there was virtually no visible smoke. Some of the picketers came over and we got all the wood sorted out. There was a blue tarp lying nearby, I grabbed it and threw over what was left of the chicken coop. I said it's better not to throw any of this in the barrel unless it's blazing hot and it's even better if that were at night. The picket captain said okay we got it.

I stopped back a few days later there was no smoke and no signs of the chicken coop and we moved on. That was the last burn barrel smoke complaint I heard of. Morris and I had built about half the stoves in use but others were very creative. I had been visiting as many sites as I could and I even got down to Portland to visit their line and give the picketers an update at a meeting hosted at the local Machinists' hall. I saw lots of variations of the home built enclosed stoves. At one site they had a cast iron pot-bellied stove and at another, someone set up one of the living room style wood stoves.

A few final thoughts about the SPEEA burn barrels. They did become an icon on our picket lines mainly because they were unique to our strike. The image of a picketer holding a "No Nerds - No Birds" sign became a staple in the media. The hinged lid made a satisfying "kerchunk" sound when opened and closed. When Boeing sent out letters advising strikers how good their contract offer was or took out a full-page ad in the paper all you heard the next day was the "kerchunk" of the burn barrel lid when strikers showed up for their picket shift and threw the letter or paper in the burn barrel. They also helped keep the picket sites clean by making all those pizza and donut boxes disappear. One day cleaning up I found a dozen rock hard glazed donuts. "Kerchunk" into the burn barrel and I saw flame leap 6 feet out of the chimney.

It was a mild and pleasant weekend as we headed into our fifth week of the strike. Betty wanted to join me on an all day picket line tour. We drove to Fredrickson and then worked our way north to Boeing headquarters. There were only a few picketers there around 9 a.m. but they were in good spirits. One of the picketers was the happiest guy I met during the strike. He had a big boom box playing classic rock and was dancing to it. We talked with him for over an hour. He had Betty laughing the whole time with his stories. I thought if this is what it's like going into the second month we could be out here forever.

We finally got up to Boeing Commercial Aircraft headquarters in Longacres in the afternoon. There was a large number of picketers on the line. As soon as we parked and got closer I saw them. There was a family all dressed as characters from the Star Wars movies. The costumes were amazing. Somebody had put a lot of effort into creating these. Princess Leia and Luke were about the same height as Betty and I respectively. Chewbacca and Darth Vader were much shorter but the Ewok was full size, one meter tall. I didn't get a chance to talk with the couple but just the way the costumes were detailed and fitted convinced me they were handmade. The most striking was the youngest child who was dressed as an Ewok.

I'm sure some observers watching us might think we don't take the strike seriously whatever that means. For the last month, there have been Dilbert costumes, funny signs and lots of music. From what I have seen so far I think the strikers take their commitment very seriously and maintain the line with good humor and grace. This has been a financial burden for everyone on the line, yet here they are. The day we went out I had three daughters in three different colleges. We had already paid tuition, room and board and all fees for the winter quarter so we're good for now. When it's time to pay up for the Spring quarter, we'll figure it out.

CHAPTER 7

FIFTH WEEK

The start of the fifth week on the lines was a warm day and thankfully no rain. We only had a few days so far of really stormy weather. On those bad days only the diehards showed up for picket duty but that was completely understandable. When I checked in at headquarters I found out that everything was in place for the rally at the Mercer

Arena in Seattle. Richard Trumka had stayed in contact with us for a lot of reasons. Now he was coming to Seattle to see our strike in action for himself. He would be the featured speaker at the rally. The fact that we were regularly featured in the national news media was hard to ignore. There weren't any visible signs of the strike faltering but we had been at it for a month and it surely was taking a toll on some of the strikers. Now was a good time to rally the troops.

Notices for the Mercer Arena rally were printed and were being sent to all the picket sites Monday morning. The Mercer Arena was in a good location with easy freeway access and would handle about 8,000 people. We had reserved a conference room in Trumka's hotel and the negotiating team and staff would meet with him tomorrow afternoon before the rally.

I went back to the lines and spent the whole day listening to the strikers and encouraging people to show up at the rally. It was around noon as I was taking a long walk around the Kent Space Center with my picket sign that I saw something I didn't expect. A woman striker was about a block away coming toward me keeping up a brisk pace. She would frequently pause when a car approached, wave her sign in the air, and if the driver honked the horn she would wave in acknowledgment. When she finally got close enough I recognized her. Mary was the last person I thought would still be picketing after a month on the line.

The last time I saw Mary was back in early February when the second contract offer was rejected. I had been spending some time meeting with members to gauge the willingness to strike for as long as it would take. Mary was a drafter and her area was a sea of drafting tables and drawing files. Scattered around were desks jammed between the tables and many had pro-union signs and posters on display. Hand drafting was becoming a dying art. Computer-aided design was in its infancy and Boeing still relied on hand-inked Mylar drawings for every part of the airplanes they built. I knew Mary and had worked with her because she did some of my drawings.

Mary had about 20 years at Boeing and was a single mother of an adult daughter. Her job was very important to her. Although drafters weren't the highest-paid employees she was able to provide for herself and daughter reasonably well. The medical coverage, vacation, sick leave, and retirement plans at Boeing were always considered to be benchmarks in the local workforce. I liked working with Mary, she was quiet, reserved and hard working.

I caught up with Mary at her drafting table and asked her what she thought about the strike. She told me it was hard for her supporting herself and her daughter on a single income. She was worried about the contract offer because she would wind up paying a lot more for medical premiums. The reduction in the other benefits is going to make it harder for her to plan for retirement. She told me that most of the people she knows feel the same way and they think the only way to turn this around is to call the strike.

Mary thought she could stay out for up to a week. I wasn't surprised at that since this is exactly what our surveys had been showing. This was the question that haunted us going into the strike. Maybe everybody would walk out but would most of them come back to work the next Monday? Standing around in the rain on the picket line gets old pretty fast. This is what we worried about and Boeing had counted on it. After all, we had never called for an indefinite strike before and there was no reason to believe some cataclysmic event had changed everything. But it had, and what changed it was those two crappy contract offers and the growing resentment of Boeing's arrogance. I told Mary all we can ask is that everybody does what they can. If she can only stay out for a week, so be it and no one will blame her if she has to go back. I also told her we are going to do everything we can to help the strikers and end the strike as soon as possible.

When I got up close I could see that this wasn't the same demure Mary I last saw standing by her drafting table. She was animated, boisterous and loud. The first thing she said to me was "I'm not going back until those *deleted* give us a fair contract." While we were catching up on developments she would wave her picket sign at every passing car and when they honked, she waved back.

Mary was definitely a firecracker out on that picket

line. I had to blink and rub my eyes to be sure this was really the same Mary. After a month on the line I was surprised how she had kept up her resolve. She was more energized after a month than most were on the first day of the strike. I was still cautious as I spent time on the lines that day but I didn't see any signs of wavering in the commitment to win this. Boeing's announcement that strikers who return to work will receive an immediate 2% raise seemed to be having no effect.

I spent the rest of the day visiting all the sites south of Seattle. It was already dark by the time I got up to Boeing Field. The picketers were still energized and there was a lot of discussion about tomorrow's rally. There were still questions about Boeing's declaration of a bargaining impasse. I spent some time explaining everything I knew and what I had been telling people was this was a legal maneuver to allow them to impose the contract terms of the last offer however they wanted. This always generated a lot of questions but I told them if we hold the line Boeing will have to come back to the table and negotiate an agreement.

It was later than I thought but since I would go right past headquarters on the way home I decided to stop by and check in. It was almost midnight but as usual, all the lights were on and there were cars in the parking lot. The phones were answered 24 hours a day by volunteers on 4-hour shifts. If a striker had a question or a problem, we were there to help. The picket site service vans ran 24 hours a day and a driver was in the kitchen making coffee for the big coffee urn in the van. The van would be restocked and head out to its assigned route. It was our plan that every picket shift at every picket site would be visited by a van. We had very reliable volunteers that kept it going and we usually had three vans on the road. That proved to be one of the reasons this strike was holding solid after a month. Everybody was connected and kept up-to-date every day.

Our public relations guy Bill was working late on the latest press release about tomorrow's rally. Before the strike, we didn't have a full-time communications staff but we needed help now so we contracted with Bill's public relations firm to keep the members up to date. There was someone I hadn't seen before. I met John who was at a computer working on some emails. He came out with Trumka to help us with strike logistics. We were also getting a lot of help from IFPTE Local 17 who loaned us staff for the duration.

There was a lot going on behind the scenes and it wasn't very visible but when you were on the line late at night or early in the morning when the service van showed up with hot coffee and news, you knew we were watching out for each other. This was the solidarity that grew out of this strike. All during the day now strikers came in to our food banks and there was somebody there to help them. If it was a financial emergency they got help getting a grant from the strike fund or a referral to community services.

The amazing thing to me was after a month how well things were running. This happened because this actually was an organic self-organizing phenomenon. There wasn't any big management structure directing every detail, it was mostly when something needed to be done there always seemed to be someone who stepped up and decided to do it. I know not everyone showed up for their picket shift and fewer still were volunteering every day but enough were. Some strikers got full- or part-time jobs and never showed up but if they didn't cross the picket line, they were supporting the strike and that was okay with me.

Since I didn't get home until around 2 a.m. I didn't get an early start on the picket lines. Trumka was scheduled to visit our picket lines in the morning and then meet with the staff and negotiation teams before the rally. I asked Betty if she wanted to go to the rally and she said she wouldn't miss it for the world. I said I was going to try and catch up with one of Trumka's picket line visits and then I would go to the strategy meeting and I'd be back by 5 p.m.

to pick her up.

Rich Trumka in Seattle

I never caught up with Trumka since he went up to Everett to join the picketers for a big hotdog feed but I spent all that time at various sites working my way up to Seattle. It was time for the meeting and I was right on time as I pulled into the underground parking. I got up to the lobby and met a few of the team on their way to the conference room. There was a big coffee urn and a stack of cups, we were set for whatever was going to happen. We were milling around when the rest showed up including Trumka. He was smiling and we thanked him for coming to Seattle. He responded that he was honored that we would invite him to address the picketers at our rally. He had never met all of us face-to-face but we'd had several conference calls with him and he generally knew who we were. Everybody got coffee and we assembled around the large conference table.

We went around the table and briefly introduced ourselves, described what our roles were and how we were supporting the strike. There was an informal update followed by a discussion of where we are now. Trumka was very well briefed by the IFPTE before he got here and he was following our strike very closely. His questions were specific and pointed. He remembered me from the conference call and said he didn't expect to find a former miner on a Boeing picket line and I told him there are actually a few of us.

The questions and discussion had died down and Trumka took the floor and said alright I've got a pretty good idea where you are and now I'd like to give you some advice and offer some help. We were ready to listen and nobody was going to interrupt him, he had the floor and our undivided attention.

He started out by saying that he had called a lot of strikes and spent a lot of time on picket lines but he was impressed by our strike. In fact, the whole leadership at the AFL-CIO was following the strike very closely. He admitted that when he met with John Sweeney to recommend that the AFL-CIO endorse our strike he was questioned carefully by Sweeney. Sweeney asked him if this was the same group of white-collar workers that had just affiliated with organized labor and had no history of a protracted labor action. Trumka told him yes this was the same group.

He then told us when Sweeney seemed a little skeptical and asked him how long we had been in the house of labor, he had to tell Sweeney, "Counting today, three months." He went on to say after talking with us on that long conference call he was convinced we had the fire to carry this out and everything he had seen so far proved he wasn't wrong. He then went on to say he was pleased that he could provide some more meaningful help to the strikers. He was donating $50,000 to our strike fund and in addition, the Communications Workers of America (CWA) was donating $25,000 and they would donate that sum every week for the duration of the strike.

We were momentarily speechless. Our strike fund had been growing but the money was being distributed about as fast as it came in. Our sister union IFPTE Local 17 had donated $5,000, which I think was the largest single donation up to now. Most of the donations were small sums although I was once given $200 by a Boeing manager. We had received a total of over $120,000 and this was a big help since the financial strain was really hard for many strikers. We thanked him profusely for the help and he said it's not that much but you have earned every penny of it and more.

Trumka waited for the chatter to die down and got serious with us. He said now I want you to listen to me carefully. You have demonstrated you know how to conduct a successful strike. You called the strike and they're out on the line right now. Then he added, "Now your most important job is to end the strike. Your people will run out of money before the company does and that's always the way it works."

The room was quiet for a minute or two while what he said sank in. He then told us that right now Boeing was talking their impasse crap and how they will implement the last offer but that won't matter unless you let it. You need to keep ramping up the pressure and I can help you do that if you want me to. He went on to say that he can help bring Boeing back to the table by ratcheting it up until they finally realize that the only way to settle this strike is at the bargaining table. He asked us if he could do that for us and we told him to go ahead.

There was some spirited roundtable discussion after that and we all got a chance to weigh in. I asked Trumka what was the duty of a negotiator. I pointed out my experience in three bargaining sessions with Boeing. The first was when we told the members to reject the offer and they did, the second was we recommended they accept and they didn't, the third time we didn't even let the members decide. Trumka said, "Your job as a negotiator is simple, when you have negotiated the best deal you think you can get and that means you grabbed those bastards by the ankles and shook them up and down until their last nickel bounced off the table, then you take it out to the members. You tell them this is the best offer we can get and if it's not good enough, what are you going to do about it?"

Trumka was right about building the pressure. To-day the New York Times ran a front-page story ti-tled "Boeing's Brains Develop Brawn On Picket Line." CBS News ran a story about Trumka's visit to the SPEEA picket lines and quoted Alan Mulally, President of Boeing Commercial Aircraft, as saying, "We are implementing the last best offer we made to our team because it's time to move forward" and they quoted me, "We're not coming back until they sit down with us and negotiate this contract." I won't belabor the point but we know how that turned out.

The meeting wound down and we said everything we needed to say. We all headed out to get ready for the big rally and I was on my way south to pick up Betty.

Rally on Mercer Street

It was dark pulling into the parking garage on Mer-cer Street, we thought were early but there was al-ready a big crowd out on the sidewalk in front of the arena. Cars had already filled most of the garage and we had to park on the top floor. It was clear we weren't that early. We headed across the street and into the arena. It was full, I didn't see an empty seat and people were lining up in the back. I had a seat up on the stage and I found a spot for Betty in the wings on one side of the stage. This was I suppose the VIP section, and it was packed with spouses, kids, overflow staff and guests. I also noticed John, Trumka's coordinator standing in the wing watching the crowd.

I looked out at that crowd and I was impressed, we did fill the place and the atmosphere was electric. We had opening remarks from our President and a few of the officers and the negotiation team chairs. Then it was time for Trumka. When he got to the podium, he looked directly at the crowd and said, "Brothers and sisters, I am here to offer help from all of organized labor in your struggle." He got a wild reception with lots of cheering and applause. He was in his element and he wasn't disappointing. He is a great speaker. He captivated that crowd, he was like an old-time revival meeting preacher. He had them cheering and stamping their feet. It really was a spellbinding performance. When he got to the point he was going to announce the donations he pulled a check out of his jacket pocket and held it in his upraised hand and said, "I've brought 50,000 dollars with me for your strike fund" and then he reached in his pocket again and brought out another check and continued, "the CWA also sent a check for 25,000 dollars and they'll send another one every week this strike continues."

I thought the roof was going to blow off the place after that. The crowd went wild. If we needed anything to perk up the strikers after a month on the line, this was it. Even though I knew everything that was going to happen I was caught up in the emotion of the moment. It actually took a few minutes for the crowd to settle down. In the back of my mind, I knew somebody out there would be calling back to Boeing as soon as the meeting was over. I thought if you think we're losing our will to tough it out until we bring you back to the table, think again. We're just hitting our stride.

Trumka wrapped it up by moving closer to the microphone, paused and then making eye contact with every person in that arena said "We'll stand with you. We'll fight with you until we WIN with you." That's all it took the crowd erupted in cheers. The rally was over, there wasn't anything more to say.

I looked over to the wings and saw Betty working her way towards me. The pandemonium was dying down and thousands were filing towards the exits. We all shook hands and everyone agreed this rally was a success beyond our expectations. We all split up and merged with the mob filing out. When we got out to the street, it was clear nobody was going anywhere right away. Cars were backed up for blocks and it seemed the whole parking garage was trying to merge into the gridlocked streets.

I don't remember exactly how or when it started but

a few cars started honking. Then a few of the departing strikers started waving strike signs out the car windows. Within a minute or two, all these cars for blocks were inching along, blowing their horns and waving SPEEA strike signs out the windows. This started reverberating in that concrete canyon which caused even more cars to join in. The whole scene quickly became surreal and we were all caught up in it.

I looked around and there were thousands of strikers on both sides of the street for blocks. I looked at Betty and she was weeping. She had rivulets of tears streaming down both cheeks. This was an emotional event and made it clear that the resolve to win this battle wasn't only whipped up by Trumka. The resolve shown by us had been honed to a razor's edge by standing out on the picket line for a month. When Richard Barnes told us last month that this was no longer a logical process but it was now driven by emotion, I didn't fully appreciate what that would look like until now.

Wednesday, March 8: Boeing stock hits a 52 week low, closing at $33.38 but our Strike Relief fund crossed through $300,000. A month into the strike the routine of maintaining the picket lines continues for the regular picketers. I don't see any noticeable changes and I go out to the lines every day. I'm getting to recognize more and more of the picketers and many certainly recognize me.

Although the news has quieted down after the Mercer rally, here and there news trickles out about the impact the strike is having on Boeing. The Wall Street Journal analysts speculate that due to the delayed airplane deliveries the profits could be down 40% this year. From the picket sites at the three airfields Boeing uses, we can see the planes stacking up. And although not strike-related, on Saturday a Sea Launch rocket carrying a $100 million satellite falls into the ocean, more bad news about Boeing.

The week wraps up in the local papers with stories about Boeing engineers leaving the company for higher-paying jobs elsewhere. The ones who stayed are still showing up for their picket shifts.

CHAPTER 8

THE LAST WEEK

Monday morning, March 13 is day 34 of the strike. The weekend was quiet but the sites remained active and engaged. This strike has become entrenched, and everyone I talked with was resolved to stick it out. As I continued to visit the picket sites every day I began to wonder how long this will last. This week would be another missed payday and I had no doubt that this would only get harder each day we're out here.

Today Alan Mulally sent a letter to all Boeing Commercial Airplane Group employees accusing some individuals of deliberately attempting to damage Boeing's reputation. In the letter he wrote, "Everyone associated with Boeing is affected by our strike situation. All of us are feeling the effects of the strike and each of us is reacting in different ways." He went on to say, "Please do not become one of the few who are maliciously attacking our company and deliberately trying to destroy our reputation."

He did not accuse SPEEA of mounting this campaign and later a company spokesman stated that, "We don't believe this is an organized thing. We believe there are only a few individuals who are actively attacking our reputation." The negotiation team did agree to increase the pressure on Boeing to return to the bargaining table and we also accepted Trumka's offer to help. We didn't realize exactly how that would look but at some level, it was getting under Boeing's skin.

That night on the picket line I saw the first indications that the "As Long As It Takes" motto was probably not realistic and Trumka was right, We have to work a lot harder to end the strike. Although the picketers were there in the usual numbers there was a more subdued atmosphere. I was approached by one of the women technicians I knew and she wanted to know how long this was going to last.

She was visibly upset and told me about the struggle she was having. She had received help from her parents and brother but was running out of options. She also told me that she didn't want to keep going back to them because it was not so easy for them right now. I gave her my best assessment which was I honestly didn't know how much longer this would last. At that point, she started weeping and it became quite uncontrollable. I just stood there with her until she regained some composure. While I waited I couldn't help feeling responsible to a certain extent. Although she decided to walk out on her own, I did everything possible I could to convince her to strike for as long as it takes. In the dark near the burn barrel with the rain gently falling we talked for a while longer. She told me with a faint smile that she could hold out another week but after that, she would have to cross the line. I told her if that's what you have to do no one will think any the less of you for it, especially me. When she walked away I felt like somebody had kicked me in the stomach.

Job fair today

Tuesday we had organized a job fair at Seattle Center. We had a big turn out and the line at registration was three blocks long. There were many local employers looking for both full-time and part-time help. There were also a few out of area employers looking to raid Boeing's skilled high tech workforce. I don't know how many people found work. Boeing told the press that 1200 employees crossed the picket line and came back to work Monday. Nobody could verify that but there didn't seem to be fewer people at the picket lines.

I was on my daily picket line tour all day and things

were routine. I visited Auburn, Kent and Renton. It was dark again when I got home. I put 12 hours on the line again today rather than the usual 8 hours at Boeing. Actually, overtime is a big part of the Boeing work culture. Most of the people I know are willing to put in the overtime when it is needed. The techs get time and a half pay since they are hourly employees. Engineers at most other companies don't get overtime since they are salaried employees. Thanks to our union contract, engineers at Boeing get paid for their overtime, which is unusual for a large manufacturing company.

On Wednesday morning I went to the Kent site early. I wanted to see how the first shift was doing. They had fresh coffee and donuts, I think I knew everybody on the picket site by then. It was actually very relaxing. This is when I noticed I was hearing "When will this strike end?" more often. It seemed more people were asking about and hoping for some progress on day 36. Everybody was now keeping track of the days, but they were willing to soldier on as needed.

We were planning three membership meetings for Thursday so I wanted to check with headquarters in Tukwila to get my assignment. The meeting flyer listed the three topics to be covered: hear the latest update on the strike and our "and more" campaign, discuss the situation with Wichita negotiations and lastly, discuss what our plans are to win this strike.

The final negotiation

When I got there I was informed there was a negotiation team meeting going on upstairs. I went up and found the meeting in an empty office. I went in and one of the staff asked me to please close the door. Some of the negotiation team and a few of the negotiation support staff were there. I asked Linda, who was there, what was going on. She told me that Charlie, Stan, Doug and Phyllis left on a plane yesterday to Washington D.C. Stan and Doug were the only two elected negotiation team members sent to the final negotiation meeting. We had gotten a call yesterday from Paul Almeida, IFPTE President, that Boeing wants to settle. Richard Barnes wanted the key principles in D.C. for a preliminary meeting today with Trumka.

We didn't get any notice about the meeting or why it was on the east coast. I asked Linda why the meeting was on the east coast and she said she had no idea, this was the first she had heard of it. No one else had any additional information, so we would have to wait to find out what was going on. The office had gotten a call from Charlie to round the rest of us up and stand by.

It's hard to know what finally convinced Boeing it was time to end the strike. It's not like they didn't want the strike to end, but until now they had not been willing to make any concessions to our demands. We knew that Barnes had been calling Boeing and pressuring them to come back to the table and settle the strike. We had been pressing our campaign to influence the FAA and the investment community. We had no idea what Trumka was doing but something had changed. What we did know now was Boeing had contacted Barnes and essentially said, "Set it up, we want to settle the strike."

How Trumka wound up as our chief negotiator was never made clear but we were asked if we would accept his help and we said yes. At this point, all of us were willing to use whatever means necessary to get a settlement for the members that would be acceptable to them. How it would all play out still wasn't clear. The away team was going to huddle with Barnes. Later they met with the IFPTE leadership and Trumka. The meeting with Boeing was scheduled later that day. We were requested by the away team to be available all day for updates and consultation.

That some of the negotiation team and a few key staff were hiding out in an empty office with the door closed raised some eyebrows. A few of the other staff wondered why some of the negotiation team were meeting privately and the rest were nowhere to be found. We sat around drinking coffee waiting to hear from the east coast.

Eventually, the call came in because there was a break in the negotiating session. We learned that at this point the negotiations were between Jim Dagnon, Boeing's head of Human Relations and Rich Trumka, Secretary-Treasurer of the AFL-CIO representing SPEEA. They were going head to head and Stan said it got pretty heated at times. Boeing had basically offered a contract with none of the takeaways which set off the whole strike. Trumka wouldn't let up on Dagnon until Boeing added bonus money and an agreement to allow agency fee, which is also known as "closed shop." The Machinists had it at Boeing and now we wanted it. That was all for now, Boeing had called for a caucus and they told Barnes they were ready to continue. We got coffee and sat around discussing the possibilities and waiting to hear what would happen next.

After an hour or two we got the call telling us that Boeing finally offered a contract proposal that we may want to accept. We sat there and could barely believe what we were hearing. Boeing had capitulated. They had removed all the objectionable parts of the original offer. No medical premiums, no change to the pension plan, guaranteed increases for the engineers, no changes to the retiree medical plans and had added bonus payments and an agency fee agreement. We went over the proposal in detail and although the bonus wasn't as much as the Machinists got, everything else was there. This is what we always said we had to have to settle this strike.

We thought about it long and hard and then we took a vote, we were going to accept this offer and take it out to the members for a vote. The negotiation team would recommend approval. The away team went back and notified the Federal Mediator and Boeing that the contract offer was accepted. We now had our work cut out for us. We decided we would not take ten days for a mail vote. We were going to arrange for live voting, and if it passed the strike would end Sunday and we could go back to work Monday. We had an enormous amount of work to do and we had three days to do it and we were on our way. Boeing emailed us a copy of the proposal and we went right to work verifying it and preparing a summary. We had the staff preparing print copies for distribution and an HTML version to post on our web site. Boeing was preparing a press release and we knew we didn't have much time. When this news hits the street, we wanted the members to have all the information. We wanted them to know why we think they should accept this offer, and end the strike.

While all the preparation was underway my assignment was to help with the evening phone bank shift. When I got down to the phone bank setup it was quiet. It was getting late and Susan, whom I knew as one of the regular volunteers, was the only other person on duty that night. That was about to change. Susan did notice around midnight that there was more activity and staff than normal and she asked me if I knew what was going on. At that point, we were only waiting for the final proofreading of our news releases and we knew Boeing was going pubic any minute. I told her we were going to announce a strike settlement offer from Boeing and the negotiation team is going to recommend approval. We are finishing the final review of the offer right now and almost ready to go public.

At 12:15 a.m. Friday, day 38, our website went live with the announcement that a tentative contract agreement with Boeing had been reached. Within a minute the phones started ringing. The phones rang for hours and people started showing up to help, others showed up just to ask questions and it was 3 a.m. in the morning. As it started to die down a little I left for home, I was exhausted. We all needed to get back tomorrow and there was a lot of work to get this wrapped up.

We had an early morning meeting and called for a Council meeting for later that morning. We proposed to the Council that we have a live vote on Sunday. After a lively debate, the council members approved the plan and endorsed the recommendation for contract acceptance. Venues were booked for three Saturday contract review meetings and the voting to take place Sunday. The SPEEA Tellers were arranging electronic voting for members not in the Seattle area. The SPEEA offices were a madhouse all day Friday until late that night. I stopped by the picket line on the way home and it was definitely not the same old routine. By then everybody had a copy of the summary offer or the whole contract in their hand. Some had the summaries we printed and others had the complete contract proposal downloaded from our website and printed at home. The pros and cons of the offer were being actively debated but from what I overheard, the pros were in the clear majority. I was already on record as recommending acceptance. There were more picketers than usual because many wanted to review the offer with the people they have been spending their time with during the last month on the line.

Saturday was going to be a big day and I was ready. Driving home I was replaying in my mind how this wrapped up and the outcome was very satisfactory in my mind. We got an offer from Boeing that had everything in it that we insisted was necessary from day one. I was expecting tomorrow to hear from people who want more, but what the hell, everybody wants more. I was prepared to advocate for the ratification and I was working through the arguments.

I still had two nagging questions in my mind, the first is why most of the negotiating team didn't hear about the last negotiation session until it was underway? The second is why did Boeing have to go to the east coast to negotiate a settlement when we were right up the street from them? The bottom line for me is none of this matters to the picketers that stood out in the cold and rain. They had stuck it out, and now it looked like all that effort was worth it.

Saturday all the newspapers had a story on the tentative agreement. The local TV and radio stations all had stories on the morning news. I was assigned to the Southcenter Theater meeting scheduled to start at 9:30 a.m. I got there about an hour ahead of time and there was a huge crowd assembling outside. They opened the doors early because it would take a while to fill that place. This was a big auditorium and it held just over a thousand. The *Seattle Times* reported that more than 2,000 workers packed the theater. When it was time to get started the place was standing room only.

When the presentation started many of the strikers had already reviewed the summary and their minds were made up. We didn't have presentation material we could project on the screen but we had stacks of the printed summaries which we handed out to everyone coming in so everyone could follow along.

The staff started presenting the offer section by section but it was more of a review because by then I think everyone in the theater had read the proposal. Then the members of the negotiation team got up in front of the microphone to answer questions. It was my turn and I found out you really can't see more than a few rows of faces because of the spotlights and there I was in the spotlight.

The questions were all over the map some more detailed than others and I thought I was doing okay. The crowd was paying attention and I certainly didn't think they were hostile. But that was about to change. The next member came down the aisle to the microphone in front of the stage and said that he was tired of listening to all this crap, and I thought, "Here it comes, this is the guy that's not satisfied and how many are there?"

He started with his assessment of why this was a crappy offer and he got louder and more combative as he went on. It quickly became a tirade. His biggest complaint was that after all that time spent on the picket line if we accepted this offer he would be losing money. The $1000 signing bonus added to the potential productivity bonus of $1500 didn't come close to making up for his lost wages. He was getting some support now from the crowd and he concluded with something like, "This is bullshit! We should vote this piece of crap down and tell them to stick it up their ass!" There was loud agreement from the crowd, but it was a minority. He went back to his seat.

I didn't say anything for a minute and let the crowd settle down. I made eye contact with as many faces as I could see and I responded in a calm measured tone. I told the crowd this, "Sometimes it's not about the money. Last year I took my kids to Disneyland and I'm not ever going to get that money back. That money I spent is gone forever. Does that mean I shouldn't have taken the kids to Disneyland? It wasn't about the money then and it's not just about the money now." I paused and I could see some of the crowd was sympathetic to my argument. I continued, "I went out on strike because I couldn't stand the arrogance and disrespect shown in those contract offers we rejected. Boeing is not going to pay us for hours we didn't work. No company has ever paid for lost wages. What we do have is a contract that restores our respect and we can go back to work Monday. If we do decide to accept this offer, when we go back we can hold our heads up high." The crowd cheered and applauded. I was sure just with that exchange that this offer would be accepted by an overwhelming majority.

I spent a few hours on the picket line that afternoon

before heading home. From what I saw on the line this offer would be accepted and we would be back to work Monday. What I noticed was the picketers seemed to be satisfied with the offer. I did not hear anyone saying that this strike was a waste of time.

The vote

The voting was open from 9:00 a.m. to 4:00 p.m. on Sunday, day 40 of the strike. We were ready because the staff worked all day yesterday and partway through the night to get everything in place. When the polls opened at nine o'clock the members came streaming in. There were many protesters with large signs calling for rejection. Some were loud and angry, and one or two tried to disrupt the voting. This did not look like it was the sentiment of the majority, and it had no effect on the outcome. Things were slowly dying down by 4 p.m.

We took the ballot boxes back to SPEEA headquarters in Tukwila. The place was a madhouse. The local TV stations had their remote vans in the parking lot and reporters and video crews were in the back of the big meeting hall. Unnoticed except by a few was Boeing's chief negotiator. I walked over to him and said I was surprised to see him here. He remarked he was here to make sure the votes were properly counted and smiled.

When the votes were counted the head teller took

the podium and made the announcement. The contract was accepted by a 70% majority of votes. The room exploded with cheers and the results were on the eleven o'clock news and in the morning papers. The strike was over and we would return to work Monday morning. I saw John on the way out and he told me that he had covered many strikes for Trumka but this was the first without a single arrest on the picket line. He said, You guys were great!"

I stopped by the picket lines on the way home. The few picketers that were left were cleaning up the sites and putting out the fires in the burn barrels. I waited until one cooled off and loaded it in my truck. Since I built this thing, I thought I would take it home for a souvenir. Everybody left the picket sites that night and they were all empty for the first time in 40 days.

Monday, March 20

I got up that morning early, ready to go back to work and I have to admit it was a strange feeling. We all waited for 9:00 a.m. because we decided to go back to work at the same time we left work 40 days ago. Rich Trumka came back to town to join in the celebration. He was in front of the Renton main gate welcoming the workers back.

I was in the Space Center parking lot and I saw a lot of familiar faces from the picket lines as well as friends I've worked with for years. Some people were lining up for pictures with co-workers and there in the front of one group was Mary with a smile as wide as the one she had on the picket line.

Back to work

Most of the lower level managers were out in the halls when we returned and welcomed us back. When I got to my desk, I found nobody did any of my work while I was gone. This was generally true for most of us. At the beginning of the strike one analyst wrote a piece for one of the business journals explaining how employees on strike never recover their lost wages. This certainly happens to some but for many of us that wasn't true. The work had to get done and now we were working overtime to finish it.

There was some tension between the strikers and their coworkers who crossed the line. This was negotiated between individuals and some outcomes were better than others. In my own case I was transferred to a new group and the lead engineer there crossed the line every day. When I showed up he never spoke to me or made eye contact. Nine months later a sympathetic manager got me a transfer to a different group. They were all on the picket line during the strike and were happy to have me.

Made in United States
Troutdale, OR
02/18/2025

29079831R00094